CONTEMPORARY PERSPECTIVES *on* LITERACY

Mastering DIGITAL LITERACY

Heidi Hayes Jacobs
SERIES EDITOR

Marie ALCOCK

Michael L. FISHER

Steve HARGADON

Heidi HAYES JACOBS

Bill SHESKEY

Silvia ROSENTHAL TOLISANO

Solution Tree | Press

a division of

Solution Tree

555 North Morton Street
Bloomington, IN 47404
800.733.6786 (toll free) / 812.336.7700
FAX: 812.336.7790
email: info@solution-tree.com
solution-tree.com

Visit **go.solution-tree.com/21stcenturyskills** to find direct links to the many tools and resources cited in this book.

Printed in the United States of America

18 17 16 15 14   1 2 3 4 5

Library of Congress Cataloging-in-Publication Data

Mastering digital literacy / Heidi Hayes Jacobs, Marie Alcock, Michael L. Fisher, Steve Hargadon, Heidi Hayes Jacobs, Bill Sheskey, Silvia Rosenthal Tolisano.
      pages cm.
  Includes bibliographical references and index.
  ISBN 978-1-936764-54-9 (perfectbound)
  1. Educational technology--Study and teaching. 2. Technological literacy--Study and teaching. I. Jacobs, Heidi Hayes.
  LB1028.3.M326 2014
  371.33071--dc23
                          2013046288

Solution Tree
Jeffrey C. Jones, CEO
Edmund M. Ackerman, President

Solution Tree Press
President: Douglas M. Rife
Editorial Director: Lesley Bolton
Managing Production Editor: Caroline Weiss
Senior Production Editor: Edward Levy
Copy Editor: Sarah Payne-Mills
Proofreader: Elisabeth Abrams
Cover Designer: Jenn Taylor
Text Designer: Laura Kagemann
Text Compositor: Rian Anderson

In Memory

The *Contemporary Perspectives on Literacy* series is dedicated to Jane Bullowa, former assistant superintendent for instructional services at the Ulster Board of Cooperative Educational Services in upstate New York, where she worked for thirty-seven years. It has been my experience that regional service center leaders are among the most talented and forward-thinking educators in the United States. In that tradition, Jane was relentlessly progressive yet had the easiest style. She encouraged innovation and provided educators with opportunities to try out new approaches. In particular, she prompted me to engage in the integration of emerging technologies from the onset of the first CD-ROMs to Netscape Navigator as a browser. I vividly remember the day she introduced me to my first videoconference on a Polycom, and I could see the world expanding in our classrooms. Jane opened learning portals for thousands of students, teachers, and administrators. Thank you, Jane.

—Heidi Hayes Jacobs

Acknowledgments

The process of writing a book is both personal and collaborative. Many individuals contributed to the building of this series, bit by bit, page by page, experience by experience. I want to start with a deeply felt thank you to our chapter authors. Each one of them juggles multiple responsibilities, and I value and appreciate the time and effort each has invested in reflecting on, wrestling with, and defining the new literacies.

In two memorable conversations—one in Melbourne, Australia, and one in San Francisco—Douglas Rife, president of Solution Tree Press, prompted me to consider creating the four-book series *Contemporary Perspectives on Literacy*. I am grateful for the personal encouragement and coaching he has provided while concurrently displaying remarkable patience. Outside reviewers, under the direction of Solution Tree Press, gave us solid and incisive feedback on our first drafts that helped our authors rework and craft their text. The editorial staff at Solution Tree Press are of the highest quality, and we continue to appreciate their direction.

Countless numbers of teachers and administrators from around the world work diligently to bring the best to their students every day, and they have provided inspiration for our work at the Curriculum 21 Project. The faculty at Curriculum 21 has been supporting educators since 2003, and this support has been unflaggingly expansive.

In particular, I want to give a round of applause to Elisa Black and Kathy Scoli for their outstanding and meticulous editorial work preparing chapters for review. Justin Fleisher and Michele Griffin were extremely helpful in assisting me with the research for chapter 4 of *Mastering Media Literacy*, "Designing a Film Study

Curriculum and Canon." Earl Nicholas proved to be a constant anchor and creative soundboard in projects related to merging curriculum and technology.

With constant support and humor, my husband, Jeffrey, is always there for me when I take the plunge into a new project idea. As always, our adult children, Rebecca and Matt, are my ultimate inspiration.

—Heidi Hayes Jacobs, Series Editor

Solution Tree Press would like to thank the following reviewers:

Deborah P. Berrill
Professor Emeritus
School of Education and Professional Learning
Trent University
Peterborough, Ontario, Canada

Robin Jocius
PhD Candidate, Department of Teaching and Learning
Peabody College of Education and Human Development
Vanderbilt University
Nashville, Tennessee

Jayne C. Lammers
Assistant Professor, Department of Teaching and Curriculum
Director, English Education Teacher Program
Warner School of Education
University of Rochester
Rochester, New York

Thomas DeVere Wolsey
Specialization Coordinator: Literacy Programs
The Richard W. Riley College of Education and Leadership
Walden University
Minneapolis, Minnesota

Visit **go.solution-tree.com/21stcenturyskills** to find direct links to the many tools and resources cited in this book.

Table of Contents

Chapter 3.   Notes From the Revolution: Peer-Driven Social Learning Communities

By Steve Hargadon

Chapter 4.   Gaming as a Literacy: An Invitation

By Marie Alcock

About the Series Editor

Heidi Hayes Jacobs, EdD, is an internationally recognized expert in the fields of curriculum and instruction. She writes and consults on issues and practices pertaining to curriculum mapping, dynamic instruction, and 21st century strategic planning. She is president of Curriculum Designers and director of the Curriculum 21 Project, whose faculty provides professional development services and support to schools and education organizations. Featured prominently as a speaker at conferences, at workshops, and on webinars, Heidi is noted for her engaging, provocative, and forward-thinking presentations. She is an accomplished author, having published eleven books, journal articles, online media, and software platforms. Above all, Heidi views her profession as grounded in a K–12 perspective, thanks to her early years as a high school, middle school, and elementary teacher in Utah, Massachusetts, Connecticut, and New York.

Heidi completed her doctoral work at Columbia University's Teachers College, where she studied under a national Graduate Leadership Fellowship from the U.S. Department of Education. Her master's degree is from the University of Massachusetts Amherst, and she did her undergraduate studies at the University of Utah. She is married, has two adult children, and lives in Rye, New York.

To learn more about Heidi's work, visit www.curriculum21.com and follow her on Twitter @curriculum21 and @heidihayesjacob. To book Heidi Hayes Jacobs for professional development, contact pd@solution-tree.com.

Introduction

By Heidi Hayes Jacobs

To many of us, the label *21st century* conjures up visions of futuristic scenes from Isaac Asimov's writings. Indeed, labeling global, media, and digital literacies as *21st century skills* is a misnomer. In reality, these are *right now* proficiencies—*new literacies*. Even though the future has caught up with us, and the 21st century is right now, we continue to serve students in school systems that operate on a 19th century timetable and deliver a 20th century curriculum. To reference another futuristic author, our education system functions like a Jules Verne time machine, forcing our students to be time travelers between the present and the past.

Nostalgia for the good old days is pervasive in pockets of society, but it is hard to make a convincing case for going backward in the field of education. In my work with U.S. and international schools, I rarely encounter questions about whether or not we should modernize our education system; the pertinent questions are about *how* we should modernize our education system. Grappling with these questions invariably leads to discussion of three new literacies that exponentially empower us to communicate and create with immediacy: global literacy, media literacy, and digital literacy. The *Contemporary Perspectives on Literacy* four-book series is a place to cultivate the discussion of these new literacies.

There are five primary purposes of the series:

1. To clarify each new literacy to provide a basis for curriculum and instructional decision making

2. To find the relationship between traditional print and visual literacy and the three new literacies

3. To provide steps and resources to support the cultivation of each literacy in classrooms and virtual learning environments

4. To identify steps and examples of how to lead the transition from older paradigms to the integration of the three literacies in professional development

5. To inform decision makers on the far-reaching effects of policy and organizational structures on the effective modernization of learning environments

A range of perspectives is essential when examining each literacy and how it interacts with others. To that end, the series includes a cohort of writers from a variety of organizations and disciplines—classroom teachers, researchers, consultants, journalists, a media critic, media literacy and technology experts, educators from an international school, university professors, and officers of an international society supporting global learning. This team has come together to share views and experiences with the central goal of expanding and contributing to the practice of educators. The commitment of each author to this work is commendable, and I am grateful for their patience and productivity. Working with them has been a remarkable journey.

The new literacies provide exciting possibilities for classrooms, schools, organizations, and social networks. In this series, we consider the distinctive characteristics of each new literacy and how schools can integrate them.

This volume, *Mastering Digital Literacy*, explores the digital whirlwind of abundant applications and tools that our students seem to be caught up in. How can we ensure that our learners use these tools with sophistication?

In chapter 1, "Digital Masters: Becoming a Blogmaster, Annotexter, or Web Curator," Michael L. Fisher and Silvia Rosenthal Tolisano take educators from cyberdabbling to authentic mastery and outline the steps to deeper self-expression and academic excellence.

In chapter 2, "Six Curriculum Actions for Developing Digitally Literate Learners," I build on Fisher and Tolisano's view of the digital classroom and lay out specific actions to bring curriculum planning into the 21st century. These steps include creating policies that support the use of keyboarding, voice, and touch technologies—policies that have direct implications for curriculum planning. Other recommended teacher actions include tagging, creating a clearinghouse, and designing apps.

Social media is a powerful way to employ digital tools. Steve Hargadon, founder of Classroom 2.0, one of the world's largest professional learning networks, shares his extraordinary experiences in chapter 3, "Notes From the Revolution: Peer-Driven Social Learning Communities." Steve has profoundly contributed to the opening of portals for communication, community building, and creativity. In this chapter, he shares lessons he has learned working with educators around the world.

Perhaps one of the most exciting developing arenas in education is gaming. Marie Alcock, in chapter 4, "Gaming as a Literacy: An Invitation," gives the reader a guide for understanding the intention and possibilities of gaming that support positive addictive qualities in learning. Marie provides a background and context for educational game design.

Finally, in chapter 5, "The Classroom Website: A Marketplace for Learning," Bill Sheskey and Marie Alcock show educators how to extend the classroom to a teacher webpage. Given that learning is a 24-7 proposition, they provide messaging strategies to students. By posting, sharing, and gathering in compelling web-design layouts, our learners will experience the new learning marketplace. This chapter provides rich examples and details for activating digital tools.

We hope this material will bring different perspectives to the dialogue regarding how to support the shift to new types of learning environments that integrate digital, media, and global literacy into organizations, teaching practice, administrative styles, and ultimately, the lives of learners.

We encourage you to connect *Mastering Digital Literacy* with its companion books in the series for a more complete and detailed examination of the new literacies.

Visit **go.solution-tree.com/21stcenturyskills** to find direct links to the many tools and resources cited in this book.

Michael L. Fisher is an educational consultant and instructional coach, working with schools and districts around the United States and Canada to sustain curriculum-mapping initiatives and implement instructional technology. He specializes in the integration of research-based instructional strategies to facilitate transformations of curriculum design, instructional practice, and professional collaboration around 21st century fluencies, Common Core State Standards, and digital tools.

Michael has a master's degree in English education and postbaccalaureate certificates in teaching science, English language arts, and gifted education. He has taught a variety of grade levels and content areas, primarily in middle schools. He is a Curriculum 21 faculty member and an active blogger on the Curriculum 21 blog (http://curriculum21 .com/blog) and the Association for Supervision and Curriculum Development's social network EDge (http://edge.ascd.org). Michael most recently published *Upgrade Your Curriculum: Practical Ways to Transform Units and Engage Students*.

To learn more about Michael's work, visit his website, The Digigogy Collaborative (www.digigogy.com), and follow him on Twitter @fisher1000.

Silvia Rosenthal Tolisano is a Curriculum 21 faculty member who specializes in upgrading curriculum content to include skills and literacies of the 21st century. She has worked as a computer teacher, web designer, world language teacher, technology integration facilitator, and 21st century learning specialist.

Silvia's passions include globally connected learning, information visualizations, technology integration, and 21st century skills and literacies, as well as digital storytelling. She is known internationally in the edublogosphere and Twittersphere as *Langwitches*.

Born in Germany and raised in Argentina, Silvia holds a bachelor's degree in Spanish with a minor in international studies and a master's in education with an emphasis in instructional technology. She currently resides in Brazil.

To learn more about Silvia's work, visit her blog at www.langwitches.org/blog and follow her on Twitter @langwitches.

To book Michael L. Fisher or Silvia Rosenthal Tolisano for professional development, contact pd@solution-tree.com.

Chapter 1

Digital Masters: Becoming a Blogmaster, Annotexter, or Web Curator

By Michael L. Fisher and Silvia Rosenthal Tolisano

Have you ever heard of neuroinformatics? What about holography? Electronic paper screens? There is much on the horizon of education and technology, but we can't just jump from point A to point B, and we can't do everything at once. Journeys aren't taken in leaps; they are traveled in steps. We must navigate through side trips, purposeful actions, and task-specific instructional practice. We must learn to work collaboratively to discover and implement the things that will matter to students, even if they aren't yet on our radar for instructional consideration. We are obligated now to create modern environments for learning that both engage and support deep thinking.

Becoming a digital master—a digital literacy specialist—is not just about using digital tools. It is about learning to navigate the new digital horizon. It is about being willing to expand learning in multiple and previously unknown directions to reach our learning destinations. We must become problem solvers—pioneers who seek out the challenge and then rise to meet it.

To do that, we need to learn one of the most difficult lessons of modern teaching practice: relinquishing control. Information no longer lives within the teacher or even within the school. It lives everywhere, which means learning must happen everywhere. In her TED talk, Diana Laufenberg (2010), shares how she moved from a learning environment of information scarcity—the environment in which her grandmother, her father, and she herself went to school—to one of information surplus. She asks, "What do you do when the information is all around you? Why do you have kids come to school if they no longer have to come there to get the information?"

Another intriguing consideration is the relationship between illiteracy, literacy, and fluency in the digital world. How do we define each of these stages? Has the definition of each changed over time? What are its characteristics and milestones? How does one progress from one stage to another? What happens to those who remain illiterate and do not move forward?

In an attempt to investigate these questions, we will look at the foundations of literacy, explore digital beginnings and forms, and investigate the analogy of digital fluency and language fluency. We will explore what we've known for years and what we need to consider as we overhaul and transform our design and practice. We will consider an operational definition of digital literacy for the classroom and the role of blogging, annotexting, and curating as side trips on the journey to becoming a digital master. Then, we will investigate the actions that get us into the digital master zone.

Defining the Foundations of Literacy

We hear the word *literacy* everywhere in education. The dictionary defines literacy as having "knowledge or competence" and being "versed in literature or creative writing" (Merriam-Webster.com, 2013). To be literate means to be educated—able to read and write. If one lacks these abilities, he or she is *illiterate*.

Traditionally, being able to read and write triggers thoughts of printed text, signs on the street, labels on products, and so on. We think of the ability to communicate in writing—letter communication in business or the private arena and essays or research papers in an academic setting. With our lives moving more and more into a digital world, the word *literacy* has to evolve, too.

What does it mean to be literate in a world of constant and easily accessed information, social media, network tools, smartphones, and tablets? What does it mean to be able to read and write *online*? What are the consequences for a person who is *not* able to read and write online? Would we consider as literate a person not able to read and write on blogs, not able to find and communicate information and ideas on Twitter, or not able to filter and sift through hundreds of search results to find reliable resources? A *New York Times* article points out that:

> Administration officials and policy experts say they are increasingly concerned that a significant portion of the population, around 60 million people, is shut off from jobs, government services, health care and education, and that the social and economic effects of

that gap are looming larger. Persistent digital inequality—caused by the inability to afford Internet service, lack of interest or a lack of computer literacy—is also deepening racial and economic disparities in the United States, experts say. (Wyatt, 2013)

Are we in a transitional moment in history when adults can still "get by" with analog reading and writing and appear to be literate in the digital world as its communication platforms evolve? How long will it take analog readers and writers to become irrelevant? Are the choices some adults make to "not do computers," write only handwritten notes, and read only printed newspapers and books still acceptable as evidence of being literate? What will happen to almost 780,000 subscribed readers of the *New York Times* print edition when the printed paper ceases to exist, as Arthur Sulzberger, the publisher, announced it would "sometime in the future, date TBD" (Shea, 2010)? Will they switch to other printed newspapers, or will they be left without a trusted news source? Will they have to rely on other people to select and print out digital pieces for them to read on paper?

During the initial phases of the World Wide Web in the early 1990s, reading and writing seemed to have been translated from the traditional analog version into the online version with few differences. The ability to link and change content at a moment's notice added a small advantage over previous writing habits. A major shift did not take place until the advent of the so-called web 2.0 around 2004. *Web 2.0* is the "term used to describe web pages and sites that allow users to add content as well as read the information provided" (Crockett, Jukes, & Churches, 2011). Many paid and complicated programs, such as Adobe Dreamweaver, were replaced with free and easy-to-use tools like Weebly, Blogger, or WordPress, which turned more consumers into content producers.

At the same time, more and more people gained access to the digital world with cheaper computers, smartphones, and other mobile devices. An explosion of online content spurred communication of ideas, information overload, documentation of current or personal events, networking, global connections, social interactions, worries about how to act responsibly in the new digital world, and all kinds of new media. The notion of reading and writing in terms of literacy has had to expand to accommodate these new kinds of online interactions and forms. The notion of literacy must now go beyond basic literacies and include network literacy, global literacy, information literacy, media literacy, and digital citizenship.

Just as basic literacy is comprised of different levels of sophistication around reading and writing, digital literacies follow a similar path of increasingly sophisticated purposes, capacities, and competencies whose characteristics we don't yet fully know. Our digital world is not fully explored; it is constantly changing, growing, expanding, and being reinvented. There are purposes and problems of which we are not even aware. However, we do know that in order to remain relevant and literate in the future, we must increase our abilities beyond traditional, basic literacy. As Lee Crockett, Ian Jukes, and Andrew Churches (2011) state in their book *Literacy Is Not Enough*, "We need to rethink what our definition of literate is, because a person who is literate by the standards of the 20th century may be illiterate in the culture of the 21st century" (p. 57).

Becoming literate in the digital world as an adult is a choice each of us has to make. Since we did not grow up with the technology, we have to make a conscious decision to learn about and experience it. As teachers, we are charged with educating our students for their future, not our past. Plenty of educators say, "I don't do computers; I am literate in an analog world. I *choose* not to venture out and participate in the digital world." Note the distinction made here between *literacy* and *digital literacy*. As part of the larger picture in education, can we even allow classroom teachers, curriculum writers, administrators, superintendents, and educational policy makers to make such a distinction any longer?

In his book *Why School? How Education Must Change When Learning and Information Are Everywhere*, Will Richardson (2012) paraphrases psychologist Herbert Gerjuoy's often quoted observation that the illiterate of the 21st century will not be those who cannot read and write, but those who cannot learn, *unlearn*, and relearn. The ability to learn, unlearn, and relearn is key to succeeding in the exponentially changing digital landscape. Educators need to model that process for their students constantly, transparently, and vigorously. Richardson and Gerjuoy are not the only ones emphasizing learning as *the* essential skill for the 21st century. As Donald J. Leu Jr. (n.d.) of Syracuse University points out:

> Regular change is a defining characteristic of the new literacies. This simple observation has profound consequences for literacy and literacy education. The continuously changing technologies of literacy mean that we must help children learn how to learn new technologies of literacy. In fact, the ability to learn continuously changing technologies may be a more critical target than learning any particular technology of literacy itself.

This does not mean simply learning particular software programs but implies the ability to think critically, solve problems, adapt to situations, transfer previously learned skills to different platforms, overcome obstacles, and navigate new landscapes fluently. *Fluency* is usually used in a language context to connote the ability to express oneself easily, but we like the way it is used on the 21st Century Fluency Project (2013) site:

> The 21st Century Fluencies are not about technical prowess, they are critical thinking skills, and they are essential to living in this multimedia world. We call them fluencies for a reason. To be literate means to have knowledge or competence. To be fluent is something a little more; it is to demonstrate mastery and to do so unconsciously and smoothly.

We are reminded of the stages one goes through learning a foreign language—from being unable to read or write, to (hopefully) becoming fluent in speaking and interacting with other speakers. Is one considered fluent if he or she can speak but not read or write? Or if one knows a lot of vocabulary words but is unable to put them in a grammatically correct order? Or if one can participate only in a rehearsed conversation: "How are you?" "Fine, and you?" Is someone fluent if he or she needs to translate in his mind before being able to form and utter a sentence?

In the same way, becoming acquainted with learning or teaching tools—such as Skype, PowerPoint, Twitter, VoiceThread, wikis, or blogs—will not make the user capable of knowing when to use them; nor will users use them instinctively. When every step of using a tool or program becomes an effort (formatting, recording, dragging and dropping, editing, saving, inserting, posting, and so on), when obstacles become insurmountable stumbling blocks, then the user has not achieved the objective of expressing oneself or communicating. When at a loss for words, conversation stalls or becomes cumbersome.

Should we not strive to learn 21st century skills by acquiring the tools we need to become skilled? After possessing these skills, should we not push further in order to become literate—digitally literate? As we immerse ourselves in the culture of others who speak the same language, would we not then, by osmosis, become fluent—speaking without translations or hesitations, smooth and unconscious of grammatical rules? Being fluent means that the language will just sound right to your ears. It will just seem right to Skype in an expert to help your students learn about a specific subject. It will just feel right to use Google Drive (https://drive.google.com), or whatever web tool, to collaborate intuitively. Fluency will come when you just know what to do next—when you don't have to think about your next step or how you used to do it before.

In any language, there are high-frequency words that form the basis of being able to communicate. In the digital world, being able to understand and "speak" like a fluent digital citizen means having these high-frequency words in your basic lexicon. Let's take a closer look at blogging and becoming fluent as a blogmaster.

Blogging

What favor are we doing our students if their skills are at a low level of proficiency and they are able to pass a class but not communicate fluently? With the next generation of web 2.0 tools, publishing to a global audience has become easier and easier. Blogs are an integral part of web 2.0. A blog, or *weblog*, is an easily edited website that gives the power of establishing a web presence to nonprogrammers and nondesigners who are unfamiliar with HTML or PHP languages or web design. They enable prosumers to use and produce content on the web, as opposed to consumers, who merely acquire and use content without contributing. Blogging, as a platform, encourages and embraces these productive consumers, in the form of reflective writing. A *blogmaster* is one who maintains a blog, is ready to create content and share, and is open to comments from others. Blogging allows these authors the opportunity to invite others to a conversation, which becomes a continuation of their own writing or perspective. This collaboration, in addition to hyperlinked and multimedia writing, is what distinguishes blog writing from traditional written forms. The potential for educators—both for their own professional development and their students'—is enormous.

We next look at blogs as a professional development tool, a teacher tool, and a learning tool.

Blogs as a Professional Development Tool

By blogging, we mean both reading and writing blogs. Both are an integral part of being literate. Including blogs in the repertoire of professional readings, along with traditional books and professional journals, is a necessity in order to be part of a global conversation in education. The traditional form of professional development for educators—attending a drive-by workshop (no follow-up or continued conversation) or a three-credit-hour university course with a traditional cycle (lecture; read preselected books, papers, or articles; do homework; attend more lectures; and write a research paper) is outdated. The one-size-fits-all model of professional development is in need of an upgrade.

We live in times of *personalized learning*. There is a wonderful ongoing discussion in the edublogosphere, the interconnected community of educational bloggers, about the relationship of personalized learning to differentiation. Barbara Bray (2012) explains that personalization is learner-centered while differentiation is teacher-centered. Personalization is about learner's choice and action; learners are encouraged to make personal decisions about their learning. Differentiation occurs when teachers scaffold instruction to make it more accessible to students; that scaffolding could extend to small groups of learners down to an individual, depending on need. This applies not only to student learning but also to professional development for educators.

Blogging fits into the trend of moving from standardized to differentiated and personalized learning. Educators customize their own reading material, which is constantly being refreshed and updated. The end of an article or the end of a book does not mean the end of reading any more about it. Hyperlinked and connected blog posts dig deeper to include further perspectives and resources. Reading blog posts provides social reading experiences that transcend geographic boundaries and connect across time. Suppose you read an engaging blog post a colleague recommended. The post mentions an article that documents an Australian educator's research and also cites a book. In the comments section, someone links to his own research, and another reader embeds a video of an interview with the book the blog writer cited. Through the conversation on the blog, a video conference is set up between the blogger, book author, and some of the commenters to discuss their experiences, examples, perspectives, and future plans. Traditional reading materials could not provide this experience. We ride a fluid wave according to our interests and needs.

Technophobic teachers immediately equate blogging with technology and become defensive. If they dig a little deeper, however, they would see that blogging is more about writing than technology. If they dig even deeper, they will discover that blogging starts with reading (Shareski, 2008).

Blogs as a Teacher Tool

Becoming an avid blog reader is the first step for a teacher contemplating blogging with his or her students. Reading blogs with metacognitive analysis in mind will also expose teachers to the potential that blogging holds in relationship to learning. To customize this new reading experience, we use tools, such as RSS (Real Simple Syndication) readers, which make accessing, saving, organizing, and sharing our reading material manageable. These RSS readers allow the user to subscribe to websites that provide an RSS feed. Using the feed, users can have hundreds of subscriptions but read them all in one place. There is no longer the need to visit each site individually to check for an update.

We have had routines like reading the morning paper, curling up with a book in the afternoon, or reading another chapter before bedtime, so we know routines will allow us to incorporate new forms of reading. Try using an RSS reader, like

Feedly, that allows you to create folders to organize your feeds by topic or theme. Use a tablet, such as the iPad, with apps that create personalized magazines with RSS feeds, such as the Flipboard or Zine apps. Find ways to facilitate these new routines until they become a habit.

From using blogs as passive readers, we move on to becoming active participants in the conversations of the blogosphere. It seems a big first step for many to leave the comfort of anonymity and speak up (maybe we should say "write up") for the first time online. Taking your position in the chain of communication is another step toward literacy. It is also when we make connections with other bloggers by leaving comments and creating content, as well as experimenting with hyperlinked as opposed to traditional writing forms.

These might seem like daunting tasks for many educators; some may even question the rationale behind embedding blogging into their teaching and learning practices. We have heard an elementary classroom teacher exclaim that she could not see how writing a blog could benefit her in any way. She did not even like to write in the traditional offline form. It was shocking that an educator openly confessed to not liking to write, although she had been charged with teaching writing and instilling a love for learning in her students!

For educators, the rationale for writing a blog goes beyond writing a digital journal or honing and improving their writing skills. Blogging can be a documentation of thoughts, metacognitive analysis, reflection on the learning process, or a curation of resources. Blogging goes beyond the personal aims of the blogger and fulfills the "moral imperative of sharing" that Dean Shareski calls for in his K–12 Online Conference 2010 keynote presentation (Shareski, 2010). Blogging connects the reader and writer to a global network of educators who are thinking about and reflecting on the same kinds of topics they are. This notion of immediate connections is critical. The exponential global reach a teacher can have is something new. Imagine a teacher writing a reflective post one evening about her classroom experience that day. She posts the reflection to her blog from the comfort of her home, only to wake up the following day to see that thousands of people from around the world have read her blog post, retweeted it, and commented on it overnight.

David Jakes (2007) comments that teachers "who have kids write for the refrigerator" should take another look at the possibilities new forms of writing platforms afford. Teachers need to coach students in writing for a larger audience than their teachers and parents alone.

Blogs as a Learning Tool

In order to facilitate student blogs for learning, the teacher needs to have an understanding of blogging. This requires a pedagogical commitment—not a commitment to using a specific technology but a commitment to student learning and quality work.

Anne Davis (2007) on her Edublog *Insights* writes the following in the post "Rationale for Educational Blogging":

> It is not just a matter of transferring classroom writing into digital spaces. Teachers need to address writing for a public audience, how to cite and link and why, how to use the comment tool in pedagogical ways, how to read web materials more efficiently as well as explore other ways to consider pedagogical uses of blogs. Blogging requires us to teach students to critically engage media. Students need instruction on how to become efficient navigators in these digital spaces where they will be obtaining a majority of their information.

In fact, blogging involves a wide array of skills, including the following:

- Collaboration
- Presentation
- Communication
- Media literacy
- Technology concepts and operations
- Typing
- Writing
- Hyperlinking
- Networking
- Information literacy
- Digital citizenship literacy
- Reflection
- Publishing
- Organization
- Global awareness

- Reading

- Commenting

Blogging is not a classroom project with a predetermined beginning and end. It cannot be an add-on to a teacher's busy schedule. Making the decision to blog for student learning requires educators to think in new forms; to take a look at their curriculum, standards, and objectives; and to make direct connections to the use of blogs. Educators must learn not to transfer the old analog forms into a digital world but to translate with the fluency of a native between both worlds. Direct translation of vocabulary words, grammar rules, or idioms might end up in disaster, as any bilingual person can attest. One has to take all the customs, traditions, rituals, and set phrases into account. Culture, too, is like an iceberg: above the water, only 10 percent of it is visible (language, dress, music, literature, celebrations), while 90 percent is unseen (concept of time, personal space, rules of conduct, notions of courtesy, and so on). The same holds true for the digital landscape.

Whether it's for a classroom or personal blog, when students take ownership, they develop an understanding of how the blog is a testament to their learning journey, a documentation of their understanding at a moment in time, and their global communication hub. Over time, the blog will also turn into a curation tool of their interests, passions, reflections, schoolwork, and subjects.

As part of the translation process into the blogging world, in addition to grade-level and subject objectives, standards, and goals, we cannot leave assessments behind in the analog world. When blogging with students, the teacher is responsible for reviewing their assessments. There is not enough time in a school day to continue to test and assess students in traditional ways in addition to asking them to blog. In her book *Curriculum 21*, Heidi Hayes Jacobs (2010) suggests using an upgrade model: "The upgrade model begins with consideration of assessment types, moves to content reviews and replacement, and then links both of these to upgraded skills and proficiencies" (p. 20). How does this work in practice?

Students in a fifth-grade class at the Martin J. Gottlieb Day School in Jacksonville, Florida, are active contributors to their classroom blog, and they maintain their own digital portfolios. The teacher actively looks for opportunities to connect her students and coach them to write for an authentic global audience. She participates in *quad-blogging*, a four-week project that allows her students to write for a specific audience of three other classrooms from different countries for one week and then alternate to become the readers and commenters for the other participating classrooms for the remaining three weeks. The content of student blog posts varies to give evidence of learning from a variety of subject areas. Students use the blogs as a hub for their learning artifacts through a variety of media.

This example assesses students' abilities to write for multiple audiences. In the past, these audiences may have been in class or perhaps family members. Using technology tools, we strategically upgrade what the students are doing by teaching them skills related to blogging and interacting with international audiences. This impacts the original focus of learning around the writing skills. Additionally, because the students are responsible to each other for reading and making quality comments, they learn to revise their work based on peer analysis versus teacher analysis only.

Annotexting

One of the biggest takeaways from learning about new literacies is their interconnectedness. This is particularly true of *annotexting*, an upgrade of the traditional modes of annotating text. While annotexting works like annotating in that students read closely for explicit and implicit meanings, with annotexting, students use multiple web tools, allowing for increased opportunities for collaboration and extended group thinking, to collect notations. These extensions of group thinking go beyond the local physical groupings of students and open up possibilities for worldwide input.

In traditional classrooms, students read text, write summaries, explore vocabulary, and take multiple-choice tests on some of the big thematic elements in the text. For example, when Mike was in high school, the most in-depth assessment he took was the Advanced Placement exam, on which he was asked to do a comparative analysis of two different texts. At the time, he thought it was the hardest thing he'd ever done. Now, with decades of experience in education, he sees that assessment as just midlevel thinking.

With the advent of the Common Core State Standards—in fact, with the advent of all that modern learning means—there arise different expectations and implications for both teachers and students. We have a responsibility to make media, in any form, come alive for the experiencer. (Note that we did not just say for the *reader*.) We need to teach students to make media a contributing part of a collaborative literacy—to converse with text and to live, breathe, and become it. We need the thinking to be visible. We must collect thinking data—in this case, in the form of annotations, so we can extend and collaborate around the learning and deepen our objectives and impact. This is not necessarily new—students have been annotating text for years to explore evidence-based questioning techniques, domain-specific vocabulary, content knowledge, and evidence to support claims.

These annotations, however, are an independent activity and represent only one level of depth in the analysis of media.

THE HOW

In a blog post on the time-treasured classroom staple KWL (know, want to know, and learn) chart, Silvia Rosenthal Tolisano (2011) describes an upgrade:

> In direct relation to our quest to bring information literacy in the 21st century to our teachers and students, the "HOW will we find the information" sticks out right away for me. A chart that points out "knowing HOW to get to information," which highlights essential skills in the information age, seems of vital importance when planning lessons and units, as well as teaching the process to our students.

Here a challenge is inserted into the traditional mode of learning, which is somewhat passive. With modern technology, *how* is completely variable. Knowledge doesn't just live within the teacher or the books in the library; knowledge is, as Laufenberg (2010) notes, everywhere and accessible in multiple ways.

The how invites opportunities for multiple perspectives and collaborative ways to research, explore, analyze, and draw conclusions—exactly the intersection where annotexting lives. The college- and career-ready student is expected to attend to audience, task, purpose, and discipline in both reading and writing (NGA & CCSSO, 2012). The standards also expect students to think critically and value evidence. The document goes on to explain that the college- and career-ready student should use digital media strategically and purposefully. Annotexting combines all of these capacities (NGA & CCSSO, 2012).

Using Multiple Devices

Classrooms can use annotexting across multiple devices and platforms, utilizing web applications and device-specific apps and creating opportunities for collaborative group-constructed thinking. As Michael L. Fisher and Jeanne Tribuzzi (2012) note:

> Students could reflect on the collective evidence as a metacognitive activity to assess their own learning. Perhaps the collaborative exercise raised new questions for them or offered them new ways

of thinking about the text. Perhaps there is something else the student wants or needs to know?

An example could be a discussion of William Blake's poem *The Tyger*, originally published in 1794. Students could use a web tool, such as NoteApp (http://noteapp.com), to discuss the significance of small differences between the first and last stanzas of the poem. NoteApp and similar websites like Padlet (http://padlet.com) or device apps like Infinote and Corkulous allow the user to post the digital equivalent of sticky notes on a virtual corkboard. Students can collaboratively collect important thoughts and quotes as well as recognize and respond to characters, thematic elements, and plot details. They can ask questions of the text and each other to further comprehend what they are reading. Using similar digital tools opens up opportunities for global collaborative notations and for uncovering more than students would in the traditional way.

When preparing students for college and careers, we have an obligation to nourish their capacity for group thinking and nonlinear solutions. Reading and comprehending need to become interdependent with social constructs and multiple meanings. Students need to be able to leverage social media to help them comprehend at a deeper level as well as for the sake of exploring differing perspectives and cultures. Different experiences breed different conclusions. Every opportunity for action and access to information must be explored. The only way to do that in an organized and modern way is to leverage current Internet and device-specific technologies. Sure, you could try this without technology, but we are preparing students for their world, not the one we were raised in or are comfortable with.

Social tools on the Internet enable synchronous and asynchronous global conversations about new ways of learning. Students can use any device they are comfortable with, and just about any of the popular social tools will work. Although many of them will be subject to local filtering, students are no longer limited to what might be available in just their classroom or school. The world is their classroom now.

Web tools such as TodaysMeet and Tinychat afford a quick way to create an online space to capture a conversation. These tools can be used at multiple levels—from the lower-level thinking skills, where students simply gather thoughts, to midlevels, where they start connecting to previous experiences in their lives, in other texts they've read, or to events that are happening in the world. Upper levels of thinking may also be conversational: students could speculate about inferences or dive into the text at multiple levels of analysis and evaluation. Additionally, these tools are interactive and can be shared with a small, large, or outside-of-school group or with anyone in the world with the specific link that is generated when you create a room in one of these services.

A science teacher at Starpoint Middle School in Lockport, New York, began his 2012 unit on plate tectonics by asking students to do a close reading of a news article about earthquakes in Japan. He created a NoteApp page for each of his classes and then shared the link on his classroom website. On the website, the teacher asked several text-dependent questions that required students to give detailed evidence to support their answers to questions. As part of their home-work, the students recorded their answers, along with the paragraph in which they found their answers. Students who wished to were able to use the library at school to do this, depending on time commitments or Internet access outside of school. The next day, the class collectively looked at students' digital sticky notes as pieces of evidence to help draw conclusions about the purpose of the article and the related science information regarding plate tectonics.

Exploring Other Options

Other options for engaging students in annotexting include collaborative doc-ument-creation sites like Google Drive. There are a number of ways to use such services for annotations and meaning making during reading. Students can cre-ate documents that consist of lists of items they think are important or that they want to remember. They might create multiple tables with columns that represent specific elements, such as connections, quotes, and plot details. They could then collaboratively take notes and determine priorities within the notes they've taken. Out of the collected notes, students decide collaboratively which are the most important and make decisions about keeping the important pieces and cutting the fluff.

All of this could also be done with applications that are on popular digital devices like iPads, Kindles, Droids, and more. Some of these apps, like PaperPort, Noteshelf, iAnnotate, and PhatPad, let users either import or take notes and then annotate them. In terms of collaboration, some tools are better than others, but all employ digital annotating as a modern instructional method.

Creating Knowledge Habitats

Interdependent learning creates a knowledge habitat. Each student has a niche, a role, and an experience to share, and each contributes to the full habitat of learn-ing in some way. When we invite others into the learning process, we engage stra-tegic and extended thinking and multiple perspectives for analysis and evaluation, and ultimately we get a better learning product or assessment than we may have gotten with yesteryear's instructional methods.

In a knowledge habitat, learning is a symbiotic construct. Teachers support the entire system and keep all students contributing for the benefit of all. Content, process, resources, and problem solving are part of the system and have needs for contributions from multiple students. There's a lot of value in letting students draw collaborative conclusions, especially if they are different than the conclusions we would draw as adults. Our experiences and perspectives are different. We can coach students through misconceptions without forcing them to think the way we think.

Single perspectives in the learning process reinforce linear learning models, such as the old point A to point B prescription for instruction. The 21st century, particularly in light of the Common Core, calls for us to teach students to think critically and be problem solvers—leveraging what they know to discover what they want to learn.

Curating

Curation is the skill of creating a subset of a large group of items or resources that are gathered together with discernment, contextualization, interpretation, and rationale. It is not just a collection of related items that have been gathered and shared. True curation offers the opportunity for conversation and new learning that an entire collection cannot do. Figure 1.2 (page 20) shows the differences between collecting and curating. Collecting is what students do when asked to find resources for a particular topic. Usually, what is collected are the first three or four hits on a Google search, without meaning, discernment, or connections. Curating is the critical thinker's collection, and involves several nuances that make it an independent and classroom-worthy task. As represented in the visual, curation is about more than purposeful collections. There are several other factors involved. The more factors that are considered, as one moves to the right across the image, the more certain one can be that curation is occurring, rather than just collecting.

Every few months, Mike takes his daughter to the Buffalo Museum of Science. The museum hosts various exhibits over the course of the year that cater to the explorations of the young scientists that visit. Many of their exhibits over the years have been interactive, and even the permanent exhibits are a little different each time they visit. A favorite is the rocks and minerals exhibit. Although the entire collection is not on display, a smaller subset shows gems and minerals from Western New York and Ontario. The display shows, through examples, the way

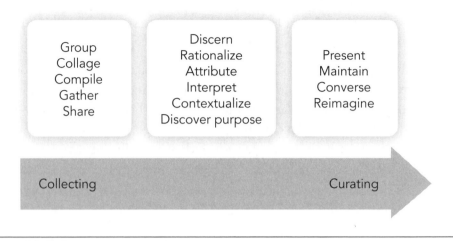

Figure 1.2: Collecting versus curating.
Source: Fisher, 2012.

that minerals form and how to identify the different types. They are artfully presented to inspire conversation, learning, and connections. A docent usually leads museum attendees through an exhibit and highlights important elements or tells a story about the exhibit. Depending on the day, you may get a different docent, and thus may have a different experience with the curated display.

Digital literacy in modern learning works very much the same way. There are myriad online tools that allow users to collect, filter, and share the vast amounts of available information, but to curate that information, we need to be able to choose the right tool and use it in a way that suggests discernment, contextualization, interpretation, and rationale.

Students are used to gathering resources, but they often present these resources as original work, without attribution. This aggregation or collection of resources does not involve new learning, new thinking, or attention to relevance or usefulness. This means that big ideas and connections are lost. To reflect their discernment, students should put some thought into what they include. They must use critical thinking and attribution. It is important for them to understand that it is OK to be a *content DJ*—remixing, cherry-picking, and creating new content from a blend of the old, so long as they observe appropriate copyright licenses. If someone else created it, a modern learner's 21st century responsibility is to give credit where credit is due, and in the appropriate way, depending on the content or the creator. Beyond those considerations, we have to go back to thinking about the exhibit, presentation, conversations, and new meanings that arise from the curated content and the docents' stories around it. How incredible would it be for students to become docents of their curated content? This could be done as reflections on the reasons for inclusion of content or connections that students are making about the curated content.

Let's look at Pinterest, a tool for collecting and organizing inspirational online content. Pinterest is more of a *visual curation* tool, but does it fulfill all of the considerations for what *curating content* means? Users save interesting content around a particular topic, but what's the rationale? What's the interpretation and contextualization? What's the new meaning and the new conversation? In essence, what's the story? Although Pinterest is a pretty cool web tool, it is more about collecting than true curating.

Why are we delving so deeply into this? Because curating is an important 21st century skill. According to the Common Core, students prepared for college and careers "comprehend as well as critique" and "use technology and digital media strategically and capably" (NGA & CCSSO, 2012). True curation covers these capacities and many more. It opens up opportunities to attend to different audiences, multiple tasks, deep content knowledge, and critical thinking. However, students have to be taught. Helping students understand the essence and value of curating content is an essential teachable moment. What do you have planned this week or this month to engage students in this level of curated collections? What opportunities lie in your professional practice to create moments for content docents to tell their stories around curated content?

Let's take a look at the student research process as an example. Students are likely to bypass traditional modes of physical research, such as using existing library books or scholarly research databases. Instead, they are apt to just google a topic. Teachers could leverage this ability to find information online by asking students to discern relevant information and rationalize the inclusion of that information in a curated way. The student research process could then be an opportunity to intersect all the skills we are advocating for in this chapter. Students could find relevant resources, blog about the justification of these sources as viable and relevant, explore each other's findings, and thoughtfully comment on those resources to further define and curate a well-focused and rationalized list of research materials.

Students might also use annotexting tools such as Google Drive and TodaysMeet or even a social bookmarking tool such as Diigo to collect resources and then, through examination, decide what resources are the most valuable. Those they retain are given a written rationale for inclusion in the curated resource. These resources could be further curated in one shareable place such as Pinterest or LiveBinders; both of these sites would allow further commenting on the resources' usefulness and relevance. Note that saving something in a service that aggregates resources does not necessarily mean that it is a curated collection.

In order for curation to be the label for the aggregated resources, there must be some sort of rationale or discernment about a particular resource's inclusion. There should be conversations around why certain resources were included over others and what, collectively, the curated resources tell us about a particular topic.

We can transform education by being cognizant of what modern students need to know and be able to do in their world. It is perfectly appropriate for us to adopt a "guide on the side" mentality in our professional practice, understanding that students should be exploring, collecting, discerning, deleting, creating, prioritizing, contextualizing, interpreting, presenting, maintaining, conversing, and telling stories around their learning.

Creating an Action Plan

The vast array of technologies and web tools available to classrooms in the 21st century is overwhelming. Some readers may already be feeling *sensory overload*. In his book *Blink*, Malcolm Gladwell (2005) argues that we may be better off with fewer choices: "If you are given too many choices, if you are forced to consider much more than your unconscious is comfortable with, you get paralyzed" (p. 142).

In their book *Switch*, Chip and Dan Heath (2011) refer to this as *decision paralysis*.

> Scene 1: A gourmet food store. The store managers have set up a table where customers can sample imported jams for free. One day, the table showcases 6 different jams. Another day, 24 jams. As you'd expect, the 24-jams display attracts more customers to stop by for a sample—but when it comes time to buy, they can't make a decision. Shoppers who saw only 6 jams on display are 10 times more likely to buy a jar of jam. (p. 51)

To minimize the feelings of being overwhelmed and shrinking your choices to a manageable few, it would be a good idea to begin considering how you will document the steps you'd take next. In order to reach our destination of becoming a digital master, we must have an action plan. That action plan must include what we are committing to and must be task dependent. At the most basic level, an implementation plan should follow these three guidelines (Heath & Heath, 2011):

1. Start with just one thing.

2. Let the task drive the decision.

3. Act more, and analyze less. (The *analyzing* phase is often more satisfying than the *doing* phase, and that's dangerous for your action plan.)

Start With Just One Thing

To avoid decision paralysis, commit to just one thing. For example, you could decide to simply start a blog. It could be for yourself or a place to share and network in a way that is reflective. Alternatively, you could begin by learning to use a tool that students could use to annotate texts digitally or to collect and curate resources, such as Diigo. Additionally, you could turn the menu over to the students and see what they build, perhaps teaching you in the process. The point is to begin by committing to just one thing.

Let the Task Drive the Decision

If, for example, you are trying to help your students communicate through writing for different audiences, tasks, and purposes, that task demands the use of technology related to writing. So, this would not be the best time to introduce students to Pinterest or teach them to use a curation tool. This would, however, be a fantastic time to introduce them to a blogging tool such as WordPress or Blogger and to teach them to leverage the capabilities of digital tools to not only communicate with each other but also to revise and edit each other's work online and share it with a global audience of peers.

Act More, and Analyze Less

Sentiments about what should be happening in education are pervasive. Politicians throw around sound bites ad nauseam, motivational speakers throw out the quote of the moment, our Facebook newsfeeds are full of inspirational educational jargon that may get some of us fired up but rarely translate into actionable steps. In short, we do an awful lot of talking about what should happen but very little about making it happen. What are the ramifications of just diving in? What are the ramifications of doing nothing? Any action that we take potentially has two outcomes: It will either work or it won't. We won't know the outcome until we try. Inaction, however, has no outcomes. Nothing has changed except for maybe the intensity with which we analyze what needs to be improved without planning for how we might improve it. This sounds like an all-or-nothing scenario, and it is, for we are too far into the 21st century for there to be any time lost wading into the ocean of modern learning. Going a step at a time is OK, but action now is necessary.

Conclusion

Becoming a digital master is essential in the 21st century educational climate. How much more time can be spent on playing catch up? Our students are there, and guess what? They still need their teachers. If our students are destined to become masters of digital literacy, someone must help them navigate that path.

The new literacies aren't meant to be stumbling blocks; they are meant to be launching pads. They offer opportunities to prepare our students for the reality of the world that they will graduate into. Our collective work is bringing us to a new intersection of informed curriculum design, enhanced instruction, and improved assessment that measures the integration of skills and knowledge versus isolated moments of content mastery.

The definition of a teacher has transformed in the 21st century. Our new titles are *guides on the side, instructional coaches, group advisors,* and *modern learning specialists.* Teacher, as a title and role, is too limiting for what educators are today. We are multifaceted and multimodal capable, with laser-sharp guidance systems that help prepare students for college, careers, and modern living. We are instructional visionaries who maintain knowledge habitats and tend the seeds of symbiotic interconnected learning. We are 21st century learners and leaders. We are digital masters.

References and Resources

21st Century Fluency Project. (2013). *21st century fluencies.* Accessed at http:// fluency21.com/fluencies.html on August 8, 2013.

Blake, W. (Ed.). (1991). *Songs of innocence and songs of experience.* New York: Dover.

Bray, B. (2012, January 22). Personalization vs. differentiation vs. individualization (chart) [Web log post]. Accessed at http://barbarabray.net/2012/01/22 /personalization-vs-differentiation-vs-individualization-chart on August 21, 2012.

Churches, A., Crockett, L., & Jukes, I. (2011). *The digital diet: Today's digital tools in small bytes.* Thousand Oaks, CA: Corwin Press.

Crockett, L., Jukes, I., & Churches, A. (2011). *Literacy is not enough: 21st century fluencies for the digital age.* Thousand Oaks, CA: Corwin Press.

Davis, A. (2007, January 17). Rationale for educational blogging [Web log post]. Accessed at http://anne.teachesme.com/2007/01/17/rationale-for-educational -blogging on August 29, 2012.

Engelhard, J. (n.d.). *His French comes out Greek.* Accessed at http://susangrosstprs.com /articles/FRENCHCOMESOUTGREEK.doc on August 22, 2012.

Fisher, M. (2012, June). Collection or curation? [Web log post]. Accessed at http:// edge.ascd.org/_Collection-or-Curation/blog/6161481/127586.html on September 14, 2012.

Fisher, M., & Tribuzzi, J. (2012, February). Annotexting [Web log post]. Accessed at http://edge.ascd.org/_ANNOTEXTING/blog/5820097/127586.html on September 4, 2012.

The Free Dictionary. (2013). *Fluent.* Accessed at www.thefreedictionary.com/fluency on August 29, 2012.

Fryer, W. (2010, February 9). Literacy is not enough: 21st century fluency for the digital age by Ian Jukes [Web log post]. Accessed at www.speedofcreativity .org/2010/02/09/literacy-is-not-enough-21st-century-fluency-for-the-digital-age-by -ian-jukes on September 21, 2012.

Gladwell, M. (2005). *Blink: The power of thinking without thinking.* New York: Little, Brown.

Heath, C., & Heath, D. (2011). *Switch: How to change things when change is hard.* New York: Crown Business.

Jacobs, H. H. (Ed.). (2010). *Curriculum 21: Essential education for a changing world.* Alexandria, VA: Association for Supervision and Curriculum Development.

Jakes, D. (2007, January 17). Re: Rationale for educational blogging [Online forum comment]. Accessed at http://anne.teachesme.com/2007/01/17/rationale-for -educational-blogging on June 5, 2013.

Laufenberg, D. (2010, December). *Diana Laufenberg: How to learn? From mistakes* [Video file]. Accessed at www.ted.com/talks/diana_laufenberg_3_ways_to_teach .html on January 29, 2012.

Leu, D. J., Jr. (n.d.). *The new literacies: Research on reading instruction with the Internet and other digital technologies.* Accessed at www.sp.uconn.edu/~djleu/newlit.html on October 2, 2012.

Lulofs, N. (2012, March). *The top U.S. newspapers for March 2012.* Accessed at http:// accessabc.wordpress.com/2012/05/01/the-top-u-s-newspapers-for-march-2012 on July 31, 2012.

Merriam-Webster.com. (2013) *Literacy.* Accessed at www.merriam-webster.com /dictionary/literate on October 16, 2013.

National Governors Association Center for Best Practices & Council of Chief State School Officers. (2012). *English language arts standards: Introduction—Students who are college and career ready in reading, writing, speaking, listening, & language.* Accessed at www.corestandards.org/ELA-Literacy/introduction/students-who-are -college-and-career-ready-in-reading-writing-speaking-listening-language on September 17, 2012.

Richardson, W. (2012). *Why school?* [Kindle version]. Accessed at www.amazon.com on January 12, 2014.

Shareski, D. (2010). *Sharing: The moral imperative by Dean Shareski* [Video file]. Accessed at www.youtube.com/watch?v=ELelPZWx7Zs on December 13, 2013.

Shea, D. (2010, September 9). Arthur Sulzberger: "We will stop printing The New York Times sometime in the future." *The Huffington Post*. Accessed at www .huffingtonpost.com/2010/09/09/arthur-sulzberger-we-will_n_710251.html on October 16, 2013.

Tolisano, S. R. (2011, July 21). Upgrade your KWL chart to the 21st century [Web log post]. Accessed at http://langwitches.org/blog/2011/07/21/upgrade-your-kwl -chart-to-the-21st-century on August 22, 2012.

Wyatt, E. (2013, August 18). Most of U.S. is wired, but millions aren't plugged in. *New York Times*. Accessed at www.nytimes.com/2013/08/19/technology /a-push-to-connect-millions-who-live-offline-to-the-internet.html?_r=0 on October 16, 2013.

Heidi Hayes Jacobs, EdD, is an internationally recognized expert in the fields of curriculum and instruction. She writes and consults on issues and practices pertaining to curriculum mapping, dynamic instruction, and 21st century strategic planning. She is president of Curriculum Designers and director of the Curriculum 21 Project, whose faculty provides professional development services and support to schools and education organizations. Featured prominently as a speaker at conferences, at workshops, and on webinars, Heidi is noted for her engaging, provocative, and forward-thinking presentations. She has published eleven books, as well as journal articles, online media, and software platforms. Above all, Heidi views her profession as grounded in a K–12 perspective thanks to her early years as a high school, middle school, and elementary teacher in Utah, Massachusetts, Connecticut, and New York.

She completed her doctoral work at Columbia University's Teachers College, where she studied under a national Graduate Leadership Fellowship from the U.S. Department of Education. Her master's degree is from the University of Massachusetts Amherst, and she did her undergraduate studies at the University of Utah. She is married, has two adult children, and lives in Rye, New York.

To learn more about Heidi's work, visit www.curriculum21.com and follow her on Twitter @curriculum21 and @heidihayesjacob.

To book Heidi Hayes Jacobs for professional development, contact pd@solution -tree.com.

Chapter 2

Six Curriculum Actions for Developing Digitally Literate Learners

By Heidi Hayes Jacobs

It is late morning, the unit of study is South America, and the fifth graders in Denise Holt's class are connected. After using the app Stack the Countries for research, Joe and Marie are creating a virtual pop-up book on the geography of South America using ZooBurst. Rachel, Winston, and Ray—gathered around a laptop in the corner of the room—are in a lively verbal exchange. The trio's charge is to tag and annotate web 2.0 digital applications that will assist class-mates in their research and project development. As they work, they refer to the class criteria that define relevant websites. Then, they tag and enter on the class website the selections on Ms. Holt's clearinghouse for the unit, which features vetted web-based resources linked directly to each unit of study. On the other side of the room, Jennifer and Dale are speaking into their tablets using Google Voice Search to gather information about the upcoming Olympic Games to be held in Rio. Sitting in a circle by the SMART Board, Ms. Holt and five of her students list questions for an 11:30 a.m. Skype call with a fifth-grade classroom in Lima, Peru.

About a ten-minute drive from Ms. Holt's elementary school is the high school her students will eventually attend. There, Carl Mendez is teaching a unit of study in his twelfth-grade journalism class on global perspectives in the news. His learners interact with their counterparts worldwide through the international student news service and social network TakingITGlobal. An added bonus for his class is that three seniors—Yvette, Darla, and Charlie—have identified this particular unit on global journalism as the focus for an app proposal to meet the new graduation requirement in the district. All seniors in their app workgroup propose an app derived from the curriculum of any course of their choosing. Mr. Mendez is delighted. He has taught journalism for twenty years, but never quite like this.

If we could interview Ms. Holt and Mr. Mendez, they would likely share that the impact of digital tools on their respective curriculum plans and corresponding instructional approaches has been dramatic. Although this is not a 1:1 district, where each student has his or her own individual computer device, building principals, using their technology budget line, have purchased tablets and laptops for classrooms to share. As exciting as the new computer hardware purchases have been, Ms. Holt and Mr. Mendez would probably share the opinion that the greatest contributing factor to their improved 21st century curriculum has been the local school board's decision to revise its policies about accessing websites and applications. Such policy decisions directly affect a teacher's curriculum choices. A new and dynamic change has also come with the addition of the new graduation performance assessment in which each student will design an app. Students and teachers are motivated to consider imaginative digital solutions.

Digital Literacy in Action

Bringing digital literacy into the life of the classroom requires curriculum and instructional translation. In order to make digital literacy teachable and, in turn, learnable, operational descriptions of what it looks like in action are necessary. This chapter will provide teachers and administrators with six actions they can use to help infuse digital literacy into curriculum plans, instructional strategies, and student learning. However, before we explain these six actions, we will explore the varying meanings of *digital literacy* in order to arrive at an operational definition for classroom practice.

Culling Through the Definitions

More than our other two literacies—media and global—digital literacy seems subject to significantly different definitions. In their article "Connecting the Digital Dots: Literacy of the 21st Century," Barbara Jones-Kavalier and Suzanne Flannigan (2006) postulate that "digital literacy represents a person's ability to perform tasks effectively in a digital environment, with 'digital' meaning information represented in numeric form and primarily for use by a computer" (p. 9).

While there is certainly evidence of *numeric form* in a classroom, the digital information students will be digesting is not limited to numbers.

A definition of *digital literacy* proposed in a New Zealand Ministry of Education research report provides an attitudinal perspective. Working with researchers from the University of Otago and Manukau Institute of Technology, Bronwyn Hegarty et al. (2010) emphasize a social and political consciousness and the necessity for collaborative approaches.

> The way in which (digital) information is used, created, and distributed demonstrates an understanding and acknowledgement of the cultural, ethical, economic, legal and social aspects of information. The digitally literate demonstrate openness, the ability to problem solve, to critically reflect, technical capability, and a willingness to collaborate and keep up to date prompted by the changing contexts in which they use information. (p. 1)

When grappling with how to bring digital literacy to our curriculum and teaching practice, we must also consider the question of career readiness. The white paper *Digital Literacy: Canada's Productivity Opportunity* (Information and Communications Technology Council [ICTC], 2010) proposes the following definition:

> Digital Literacy is taken to mean the ability to locate, organize, understand, evaluate, and create information using digital technology for a knowledge-based society. It involves a working knowledge of current high-technology, and an understanding of how it can be used. Digitally literate people can communicate and work more efficiently, especially with those who possess the same knowledge and skills. They can acquire more information and knowledge. (p. 2)

This definition focuses on the real world and has direct implications for the classroom. Teachers create opportunities for the digitally literate learner to determine when to work alone and when to work with others. Students can work collaboratively with a digital application that supports the learning experiences of students in their units and courses by, for example, creating a canvas in a small group activity on Blendspace (www.blendspace.com). There is also the added possibility for teachers to expand and to include classmates virtually. Using ePals, Twitter hashtags, Edmodo, and interactive gaming like Globaloria (www .globaloria.org), teachers can select learning opportunities for a wide array of independent and collaborative work. As Liz Ellcessor (2009) points out, there are nonreciprocal arrangements by which information is broadcast using Twitter or Instagram, meaning that there is a one-sided posting of information with no intention of obtaining a response. Conversely, teachers can also design lesson plans and activities where there is a focused group or *hyperlocal community*, as John A. McArthur (2011) refers to it, deliberately brought together for a purpose.

There are many possibilities for powerful, positive connections for our learners online, but there are equally powerful risks just a click away. A student can easily join an online social community, but there is no guarantee the site will be beneficial or assist him or her in learning. The same point applies to the general public. Ask a doctor, and he or she will tell you that the plethora of official-sounding medical sites may be dispensing frivolous advice. We have new challenges requiring new and dynamic approaches. Ultimately, the digitally literate student needs to be a sophisticated self-navigator.

Defining Classroom Implementation

Our definition of digital literacy for the classroom is as follows: Digital literacy is the proficiency to effectively employ web 2.0 applications, Internet-based tools, and repository sites to further meaningful research and development; thus, digital literacy requires four specific skill sets or capabilities.

1. **Accessing capability:** To use keyboarding, voice, and touch technologies
2. **Selection capability:** To strategically locate the appropriate application, tool, or site to match the problem at hand
3. **Curation capability:** To tag and organize source material for efficient reference, as in a personal clearinghouse of sources
4. **Creation capability:** To render new solutions and forms as seen in generating an original app design or new software platform

These four capabilities need to be nurtured and actualized in classroom practice as proficiencies. Actionable strategies are required throughout a school system, from policy to classroom practice.

Overview of the Six Actions

To implement and ensure the cultivation of these proficiencies, I propose six actions teachers and school leadership can take. These actions are distinctive and related. They start with the school leadership's decisions about what hardware to make available to students and what policies to implement regarding basic accessing skills. There are also policy choices regarding Internet safety and filtering that have direct bearing on curriculum planning.

1. **Establish discrete instructional guidelines for keyboarding, touch, and voice technologies to support the learners' access to the digital world.** School leadership needs to address curriculum policies regarding the accessing strategies necessary to gain digital literacy. Included here are decisions regarding *which* and *when*—that is, *which* accessing approach (for example, keyboarding, touch, or voice) is the focus in the curriculum, and *when* to focus on it in a student's experience from preK through grade 12.

2. **Refine and review instructional policy on Internet safety and filtering.** School and district policies on Internet safety and the filtering of specific websites exist to protect students. However, schools may need to reconsider some of these policies. Old policies may restrict reasonable and even wonderful experiences, because they are too sweeping and general. Reviewing policies is necessary to ensure that they are current and relevant, given that they directly affect teacher curriculum plans.

3. **Set criteria for viable digital application and website resource selections.** The multitude of website resources and applications for teachers can be overwhelming. In order to encourage critical examination of websites, management systems, and applications, schools can use criteria for what constitutes a viable and useful resource for the teacher and the learner. These criteria include matching form and function to the curriculum and, most importantly, determining the trustworthiness of the source or social network.

4. **Establish the proficiency of tagging applications and web resources as a critical learning outcome.** We will examine the power of *tagging*, which is labeling and categorizing applications and website resources. We will also discuss how to tag and organize applications to support student learning. In a very real sense, tagging requires critical analysis on the part of the learner and should be an important action teachers take.

5. **Curate a classroom clearinghouse to organize and match tags to units and courses.** Once students can tag sites and organize them, developing a process for curating a clearinghouse is a natural next step. A curriculum clearinghouse is an area on the teacher or student webpage that houses specific applications related to the units of study being developed. A great

benefit of this action is that the clearinghouse supports a unit or course through collaborative participation of teacher and students.

6. **Create a digital design solution project as a graduation requirement.** Whether students design a website to provide resources, create a network to solve local issues, or design an app (a software application downloaded onto a device), the goal is to support their creativity as they generate solutions to real problems using contemporary tools. When students graduate, they should not only know how to use digital tools and applications but also how to develop them. Teachers should encourage 21st century learners to be solution generators who help others solve problems with digital tools.

Whether you are a teacher, policymaker, school or district administrator, or professional developer, these six actions are doable, realistic goals that your community of learners and professionals can readily understand. Let's revisit each of them in more detail.

Establish Discrete Instructional Guidelines for Keyboarding, Touch, and Voice Technologies

School leaders and policymakers must consider two concrete issues in this regard: (1) What hardware is already available, and what should the school purchase (for example, laptops, tablets, or SMART Boards); and (2) should the school invoke a *bring your own device* (BYOD) policy?

In most U.S. and Canadian schools, you will find desktop computers and laptops in the school office, the library media center, and on the teacher's desk in the classroom. Some schools may make 1:1 purchases, so each student can access a laptop. Others have a set of rotating iPads for each grade level and a SMART Board in the media center. Many schools can now afford smaller, more efficient, and relatively inexpensive laptops like Google's Chromebook.

The disparity between learners is compounded by age and economic advantage. Some students enter school never having held a tablet or touched a laptop keyboard; others start school as confident users of these devices. Just as we screen students entering kindergarten to evaluate their social and academic competencies, I recommend we screen them to assess digital literacy as well. However, kindergarteners are not the only ones who will need screening. Elementary and secondary administrators and teachers also need to ascertain where their current student population stands on keyboarding, touch, and voice technologies. As time goes by, students will likely be increasingly proficient at younger ages, which will allow educators to focus primarily on how to help students select and employ digital tools.

Setting policy on access tools is clearly a practical and baseline action. Once our students open the doors to the resources available on the Internet and the possibilities for connecting with others, there are critical considerations. How do educators balance genuine concerns about safety and security with these remarkable new possibilities? Our next action focuses on policy actions regarding this question and its implications for curriculum planning.

Keyboarding

Throughout the 20th century until about 1990, formal typing instruction using the QWERTY keyboard method was standard but not universal in high school. During the 1950s, 1960s, and 1970s, the notion of having elementary students learn to type would have been anathema to student-centered learning. But as Ann Trubek (2011) notes, "Those classes are gone. Ironically, in our era of keyboard ubiquity, typing has fallen out of the curriculum."

The torch has now been passed from the typewriter to the computer, and the ability to use a keyboard with facility and accuracy is key to online research. More importantly, keyboarding has revolutionized writing. Many schools have designed basic word-processing instruction to include the use of toolbar features. These functions lead to desktop publishing and webpage design. Teachers can create more dynamic and engaging assignments when students can effectively use the range of writing, editing, and visual features of word-processing programs. How do we ensure that our learners are cultivating these skills in K–12?

Within the National Educational Technology Standards (NETS), the International Society for Technology in Education (ISTE, 2007) has created six overarching standards to provide an overview to support student learning: (1) creativity and innovation; (2) communication and collaboration; (3) research and information fluency; (4) critical thinking, problem solving, and decision making; (5) digital citizenship; and (6) technology operations and concepts. In particular, the sixth standard speaks to technology operations that are fundamental to developing the other five. Schools need to take action and turn these broad goals into highly discrete curriculum plans and learning outcomes and decide when to introduce and reinforce word-processing skill sets.

In examining a range of school skill sequences, I have found that it is very common to see some excellent curriculum guidelines that attempt to translate the sixth standard into curriculum practice. School guidelines might range from highly discrete, such as "Students use arrows, caps lock, return and enter, backspace, and delete" to broadly stated, such as "Students use toolbar functions effectively." Whether granular or broad in language, the question at hand is whether there are strict grade-level assumptions about keyboarding and word-processing skill development. Using strict grade-level guidelines hinders 21st century students. The precision of these guidelines is admirable, but given that so many of our learners have technology in their homes and are already agile using these tools, a second grader may be competent with a proficiency targeted for fifth grade, such as creating a sign using various fonts from the toolbar. An alternative is to maintain and update keyboarding proficiency targets but convert them into a continuum that is not grade-level specific. Students can self-assess and then demonstrate to their teachers where they stand on the continuum.

Schools can address the disparity between targeted outcomes in the two sets of guidelines by eliminating grade levels and moving to a continuum. In short, a school district should revisit and refresh guidelines to cultivate a sequence of keyboarding skills that respond to the actual student entry levels, not an arbitrary notion of grade levels. What's more, schools will need to update this sequence on an ongoing basis, given changes in the technology itself.

Differentiated keyboarding and word-processing skill sets should be the norm, because they are the reality in our classrooms. In a sixth-grade class introduced to the standard Microsoft Word editing toolbar, there might be students who are practicing the use of editing and revising functions, such as checking spelling and grammar, changing fonts, and adjusting margins. Others in the class are able to insert and track comments in their compositions and give and receive feedback in their Writers' Workshop session. Some of the students who have limited or no access to computers at their home might be learning how to create a wiki or webpage for the first time.

An actively reviewed and current continuum of skills should be the foundation of each school's digital literacy policies. Graduation requirements should ensure that our high school students are active and independent users with full command of word-processing skills and features. All of these skills rely on the ability to nimbly and reflexively press letters, numbers, and symbols on the keyboard in order to process words and make meaning from them.

Touch

One of the biggest technological shifts is the onset of the tablet, a dynamic and portable mechanism that can open up the world to users of any age. One way that tablets differ from laptops is that they approximate the size and handling of books. I believe that the iPad, released in April of 2010, became an immediate hit for that reason. It is noteworthy that Microsoft technically released the first tablet—the Tablet PC—in 1999, but because it was heavy and the size of a legal pad, it was unwieldy and did not reach widespread use. With advancements in design in the 21st century, the purchase of competitive tablets has rapidly expanded. In 2012, global shipments of tablets reached 177 million, and businesses or government agencies rather than consumers purchased 11 million of them. Of those, the vast majority were sold to schools (International Data Corporation as cited in Metz, 2012).

Given a tablet's mobility and ease of use at any age, it is no surprise that school leaders are buying them. In her article "Tablet Makers Pursue Public Schools," published in the *MIT Technology Review*, Rachel Metz (2012) notes:

> The superintendent of the Los Angeles Unified School District, the second-largest district in the country with over 640,000 students, has said he wants to have a tablet for every student and teacher by next school year. The McAllen Independent School District, located in a Texas town on the Mexican border, is handing out an iPad to each of its students in first through twelfth grades and an iPod Touch to each child in preschool or kindergarten. The cost of that project, including Wi-Fi spots and about 25,000 devices, is $20 million.

Tablets provide real opportunities for our youngest learners, even those who are too young to acquire keyboarding expertise. Carl Davis, a social studies teacher at Caston Junior/Senior High School in Fulton, Indiana, said his students use Google Earth on their iPads to zoom in and out of various terrains, and they use other programs to view the way places looked at different times in history. As he explained this, his students were at their desks, eyes glued to their iPads, embarking on a WebQuest through the Middle Ages in which they would complete a social diagram of the feudal system, observe the layout of a medieval watermill, and answer various questions (Kirk, 2013).

There is a naturalness and ease to touch technologies, and they have emerged as a form of intuitive self-navigation on handheld devices. Teachers can expect to see direct changes in their instructional approaches when they employ tablets. In a detailed and extensive Australian study, *Use of Tablet Technology in the Classroom*, the New South Wales Curriculum and Learning Innovation Centre (2012) monitored iPad initiatives in three schools in New South Wales. The report states:

> Using the iPad also resulted in an increase in students sharing digital work via the interactive whiteboard (IWB) in many instances, and this provided opportunities for the teacher to provide ongoing, just-in-time feedback and also collect cumulative assessment data. As an intuitive device, the iPad acted as a catalyst for more creative pursuits and exploration of new pedagogical approaches. (p. 9)

Note that the mobile smartphone functions as a minitablet that provides many of the same functions as tablets, although arguably, it is more difficult to read text and view images given the screen size.

Certainly, the use of all handheld devices is pervasive across generations, but there are specific needs for students, and based on demographics and home availability, touch access can begin with our youngest learners. Whether a five-year-old uses a cell phone or a tablet, he or she needs teacher support. He or she needs direction on how to use specific icons, locate and adjust the settings, determine Wi-Fi access, use the embedded keyboard features, and download books. At that point, the student is off and running.

We should also assume that there will be a range of nursery through grade 1 learners with touch access capabilities. Educators will need to rethink how to best support our youngest learners entering school. For example, does a kindergarten class just need reinforcement on using a tablet, or will the teacher be the first adult to give a student an introduction to touch technologies? Will there be students who will have had formal and extensive tablet usage prior to entering preschool? Many early childhood teachers with whom I have spoken advocate the transition to collaborative experiences on touch table-tops and SMART Boards. The table-top experience is inherently more social and group oriented, as students work together to respond to the icons on the table, in contrast to the individual and solitary experience of using a tablet.

For the preschool student in reading readiness, the use of the tablet can begin to build reading strategies, not unlike the very strong use of visual cues in a traditional reading program. For example, teachers will ask students to press on an icon, describe it, and talk about what happens. The icon has a name, such as "Wheels on the Bus," and the student repeats it. Additionally, the teacher can record the entire exchange on the tablet and replay it for the student to hear.

If the first time a student handles a tablet or smartphone is at the age of fifteen, the same basic suppositions hold about "touch and effect," but obviously the content level of an application will match the interests of the age group.

Voice

Voice technologies represent an opportunity to improve speaking and listening with immediate feedback. Curriculum policy should reflect the cultivation of articulation, commands, and directives. If we use our imaginations, we can view Google Voice Search or the iPhone voice representative Siri as another "being" who requires the speaker to be particularly clear, concise, and precise with pronunciation in order to be understood. The technology requires accurate speech from the speaker, which is in an incentive for clarity.

In truth, voice recognition technologies are not new to education or to world-language and English-as-a-second-language instruction. As Isaac Bejar (2010) states, "A confluence of developments in education worldwide suggests that *speech technology* could help to address challenges such as the development of literacy, especially reading proficiency, and the acquisition of communicative competence in English" (p. 1). An example might be for a teacher to generate for use with voice-activated search tools a list of requests that relate directly to a unit of study in the curriculum. The entire class can collaborate in the compilation of the list, sorting the entries to determine what items are pertinent. They can then carry out inquiries using "Siri" (or however the voice is named). To be clear, the majority of questions will have limited response length but they will provide feedback to the students as to the grammatical construction of each interrogative and the clarity of articulation for the speaker.

Using speech recognition tools has also been and continues to be an effective approach for assisting students with special needs. The National Center for Technology Innovation's (NCTI, 2010) technology brief reports that when a student sees a word that he has spoken appear on a computer screen, the notion of sound-symbol correspondence is reinforced. According to the report, "this bimodal presentation of text can be especially helpful for students with learning disabilities, and is thought to be why speech recognition has been found effective in remediating reading and spelling deficits" (NCTI, 2010, p. 1).

It is fair to say that in the future, the sophistication of the programming will increase, making it possible for more complex interactions with the computer. In particular, the Common Core State Standards for speaking and listening include proficiencies that classrooms can directly support through voice-activated technologies in which immediate feedback is possible. For example, see the following two kindergarten standards for speaking and listening:

> Confirm understanding of a text read aloud or information presented orally or through other media by asking and answering questions about key details and requesting clarification if something is not understood. (SL.K.2; NGA & CCSSO, 2010, p. 23)

> Ask and answer questions in order to seek help, get information, or clarify something that is not understood. (SL.K.3; NGA & CCSSO, 2010, p. 23)

Imagine a student speaking into a smartphone or tablet to give a directive, search a resource, or respond to a question. The Speaking and Listening standards in the Common Core State Standards, as well as individual state and provincial standards, provide opportunities to embed the use of voice-activated technology into the curriculum.

Refine and Review Instructional Policy on Internet Safety and Filtering

However schools choose to access digital tools and social media, there is an implicit concern about the vulnerability of students and what they might be exposed to online. As we compare digital literacy to print literacy, we can learn specific lessons from book censorship. There has always been an understandable need to protect students from material that can be harsh and disturbing. That debate usually centers on who defines the parameters of censorship and on what criteria the decisions are based.

Although North Americans value debate, discourse, and diverse points of view, banning books continues in schools, whether it is Mark Twain's *Adventures of Huckleberry Finn* or Judy Blume's *Fudge*.

But the issue of censorship in the digital age is obviated by easy access to digital material, since students can obtain books through a download as opposed to going to a bookstore or library. With the connectivity of social networking and social media comes the possibility of abuse and misuse, either by students passing on questionable images and sources to their peers with ease or, conversely, by overly censorious administrators.

Safety

The Broadband Data Improvement Act of 2008 amended the Communications Act of 1934 and brought with it extensive guidelines. For example, to receive discounts on technology purchases, elementary and secondary schools possessing computers with Internet access must submit a certification that states, as part of their Internet safety policy, that they are "educating minors about appropriate online behavior, including interacting with other individuals on social networking websites and in chat rooms and cyberbullying awareness and response."

For schools wrestling with these issues, there are abundant resources providing direction and advice, such as i-SAFE (2013), a nonprofit foundation for educators, law enforcement personnel, families, and community leaders. Founded in 1998, i-SAFE Foundation is available in all fifty U.S. states, Washington, DC, and Department of Defense Dependents Schools (www.dodea.edu) located across the world. Its mission is to educate and empower youth to make their Internet experiences safe and responsible and educate them on how to avoid dangerous, inappropriate, or unlawful online behavior. It aims to provide "pre-primary to secondary-school-level students in the United States and around the world with proactive, preventative and precautionary knowledge and means to become empowered (i.e., well-informed, safe and responsible) Internet users" (i-SAFE, 2013). The foundation's approach is a combination of K–12 curriculum materials with straightforward lesson plans and resources combined with on-site programs. The National Center for Missing and Exploited Children (www.missingkids.com) also provides established guidelines, tips, and resources in its NetSmartz Workshop (www.netsmartz.org). This educational program advocates for a proactive curriculum that provides learners with thoughtful defenses and confidence to identify suspicious Internet behavior.

Schools need to introduce Internet safety strategies early on. As Mary Beth Hertz (2012) states:

> There are three considerations when addressing Internet safety with these students. First, the transfer of handling strangers in "real life" to those in virtual environments is not automatic. It needs to be taught. Second, while most "Stranger Danger" programs teach that strangers are scary, mean and want to hurt or abduct children, this contradicts the way collaboration occurs between strangers online. Not all strangers are dangerous. Lastly, in "real life," students can walk or run away from a potential threat. In an online environment, the danger is inside a student's home and hard to escape without the necessary skills for handling tough situations.

As Hertz (2012) notes, the notion of the *stranger* is a critical focus, but schools should also give equal concern to dealing with people students already know.

A question to consider is how these concerns affect policy and the classroom. In their analysis of state laws, Sameer Hinduja and Justin W. Patchin (2013) found that forty-nine states have bullying laws, and eighteen now have cyberbullying laws. Within the school sector, there are trickle-down implications for the classroom.

Attention to cyberbullying is a major consideration in Internet safety curriculum plans. Obviously, the *cyber* prefix is attached to the larger and more pervasive problem of bullying in general. With renewed vigor, educators are struggling with effective policies to prevent potential victims and to thwart potential bullies. StopBullying (www.stopbullying.gov), a U.S. Department of Health and Human Services antibullying website, compiles and suggests specific guidelines to assist parents. This site is a useful resource for teachers to show parents, given that the most likely place for potentially unsupervised Internet use is at home.

Are we really teaching cybersafety? Are schools committed to safe practices? It is startling to read the findings of a study commissioned by the National Cyber Security Alliance (2011; www.staysafeonline.org) of U.S. K–12 teachers, information technology (IT) specialists, and administrators. The report, titled *The State of K–12 Cyberethics, Cybersafety and Cybersecurity Curriculum in the United States,* is particularly revealing: there is a notable disconnect between educators on one hand and administrators and IT specialists on the other when it comes to the success of cybereducation, as well as a school district's cybereducation requirements:

- Fifty-five percent of teachers strongly agree that cybersecurity, cybersafety, and cyberethics should be taught in schools as part of the curriculum, while more than 82 percent of administrators and 85 percent of IT specialists share those same strong sentiments.

- Thirty-three percent of teachers believe their district requires cybersafety curriculum, while 68 percent of administrators and 64 percent of IT specialists believe so.

The study also found that few teachers are educating students on basic cyberskills.

- Thirty-four percent of teachers in 2011 taught about risks tied to social networking.

- Eighteen percent of teachers have taught about dealing with alarming posts, videos, or other web content, and only 15 percent have taught about hate speech.

- Six percent of teachers have taught about the safe use of geo-location services.

- Thirty-four percent of teachers have taught about how to make decisions about sharing personal information on the Internet.

By contrast, plagiarism is the most popular topic related to cyberethics, with 47 percent of teachers reporting that they instructed on it in 2011 (National Cyber Security Alliance, 2011). One conclusion to draw from these findings is that even if there are strong intentions to focus on cybersafety, if there is no consistent school policy on integrating cyberbullying as a topic in the curriculum, teachers are not likely to teach the topic formally in the classroom.

For students, accessing skill sets is the portal to digital tools. Once students enter the portal, they will need guidance about how to search and what to search for. Thoughtful debate and discussion leading to policies for introducing digital access and safety considerations is a foundational action.

Filtering

The National Conference of State Legislatures (NCSL; www.ncsl.org) lists twenty-five states that have adopted filtering laws applicable to public schools. (Visit **go.solution-tree.com/21stcenturyskills** to view this list.) An overview of the state laws posted on the website says:

> The majority of these states simply require school boards or public libraries to adopt Internet use policies to prevent minors from gaining access to sexually explicit, obscene, or harmful materials. However, some states also require publicly funded institutions to install filtering software on library terminals or school computers. (NCSL, 2012)

The word *simply* stands out in this statement, because it is honest. It is a simple thing to make a broad and well-intended commitment, but the process of making choices about what schools should or should not block is quite complex. Support for blocking obscene and violent content is a legal responsibility for schools, and there are sophisticated systems in place, such as OpenDNS (www.opendns.com) or Lightspeed Systems (www.lightspeedsystems.com) that monitor sites parents use as well. Still, filtering is censorship, which always results in controversy.

Each school community determines the book titles it will allow or not allow in its libraries and curriculums, while recognizing that students may find what they are seeking through alternative methods. Schools make the decision title by title and not by clearing an entire genre from a bookshelf. No school would say, for example, "We will not allow fiction." In any event, it is critical that these decisions go on record. When it comes to filtering websites, a primary concern should be the misguided application of sweeping generalities that filter all social networking or blogs. The intention may be to protect, but that intention can also eliminate some wonderful resources for learners. There is no question that this is a challenging issue, but simply having blocks and bans on entire categories is not the answer. The reality is that social networking applications have profoundly increased communication production. As Clive Thompson (2013) notes, "We are now a global culture of avid writers" (p. 59). Our students need us to coach them on quality composition and the need for a safe environment, but there can be no question that they are motivated.

It is recommended that policymakers refresh their existing policies and provide an active channel for teachers to submit website and application proposals for review that are pertinent and appropriate to the curriculum. Within the parameters of a filtering policy, each classroom teacher is making daily choices and designing curriculum units, lesson plans, and assessments. How can educators strategically choose digital tools and applications that will support student learning?

Set Criteria for Viable Digital Application and Website Resource Selections

With a cell phone in one hand and a tablet in the other, the modern learner uses applications to solve problems, have fun, connect with others, and learn. Learning 24-7 with handheld devices and virtual global connectivity has replaced the agrarian classroom. How can teachers transition to an engaging and rigorous 21st century learning environment?

A wide sample of over two thousand advanced placement and National Writing Project high school teachers was interviewed in the spring of 2012 for the Pew Research Center report *How Teens Do Research in the Digital World*. Teachers consistently reported that digital tools have reduced the process of research to googling. The researchers found that teachers believe the top priority should be analyzing and determining the quality of online information. In particular, teachers should design assignments that dissuade students from simply using a search engine. Teaching students how to determine the reliability of online resources requires time that is not always readily available (Purcell et al., 2012).

The only reason a teacher should employ any technique, tool, or approach is because it works to support student learning and engagement. Does that mean we always need to upgrade to new tools? What about current instructional practice that has proved effective? Is it necessary to replace a tool with a new web 2.0 tool or a digital solution? Here are four questions to consider as you evaluate your current practice and consider digital upgrades.

1. **Does the application engage the learner in active inquiry "re-search" and promote curiosity?** Susie is a middle school student who is using Gapminder (www.gapminder.org). On this interactive webpage, she can animate statistics about each nation and its per capita income, life expectancy, and population. What excites Susie is that she can control the key variable of time; she starts watching the countries "dance" wildly on the screen from 1800 to present day. Questions naturally emerge: "What was going on in 1959 to make China dip on the graph like that? Why does Japan have the longest life expectancy? What is the relationship between the countries of South America on per capita income?" The outcome is clear. Susie is interested and continues to read and search for more answers.

2. **Does using this digital application to investigate the topic increase the depth of research?** Because it is easy to find multiple perspectives on the Internet, Johnny will not only find the information he needs, he'll have access to a much wider range of perspectives that may allow him to probe his research topic more deeply. Johnny is monitoring events in the Middle East and goes to Newspaper Map (http://newspapermap .com), where he is able to bring up hundreds of newspapers from around the world and translate them into English. He finds many points of view on the stories, but he also finds more details and different information, which provides a more complex and deeper sense of the content and issue he is studying.

3. **Does using the digital tool generate independence?** New digital tools and resources can help students develop focused independence. Rather than fostering dependencies, teachers need to coach students on independence via applications and tools that will help them improve their own work. Abdul is able to improve his writing without the teacher hovering over his work with the proverbial red pen, because his teacher has directed him to Visual Thesaurus (www.visualthesaurus.com) or Vocabulary (www.vocabulary.com), where he can revise his sentences and improve his writing on his own. Abdul's teacher suggests that he use WolframAlpha (www.wolframalpha.com) to check his mathematics on his own to not only see if his computations are accurate but to see if he might rework the steps to the solution in a different, more effective way. He uses a Khan

Academy (http://khanacademy.org) video to review how to balance an equation, and he can play the video as often as he needs.

4. **Does use of the digital tool increase student performance and quality of presentation?** Digital tools and search engines can increase student options for presenting the results of their research. Fifth graders in a school in Massachusetts replaced the poster they were going to create about Gandhi with a Blendspace canvas (http://blendspace.com) including images, a video interview, a map of the places he traveled, and a timeline of key events. There is a wide range of presentation platforms, such as Prezi (http://prezi.com), ScreenFlow (www.telestream.net/screenflow), Lucidchart (http://lucidchart.com), Little Bird Tales (https://littlebirdtales .com), or Museum Box (http://museumbox.e2bn.org). Teaching students what presentation format matches the purpose and audience is important. The eye-catching, rapid movement of Prezi's virtual whiteboard is a good choice for capturing the attention of an audience, whereas the more linear sequence of PowerPoint is useful for a sustained presentation. The combination of enhanced formats and the exponential increase in functionality for research can result in greatly improved, quality presentations.

Establish the Proficiency of Tagging Applications and Web Resources

Where do I start with digital tools? How do my students make sense of the wide array of web 2.0 applications that are out there? There is a big, wide-ranging, unorganized mess of wonderful ways to help students. What can I count on? These questions and many others came my way from educators around the world after the publication of *Curriculum 21: Essential Education for a Changing World* (Jacobs, 2010). This was a challenge unlike any other I had encountered in my career, and it occurred via email correspondence and during my workshops. There was reluctance on the part of many to try out new ideas and tools, and I observed tremendous doubt about organizing and trekking through a sea of websites and resources.

In response to this tsunami of help requests, our Curriculum 21 faculty began developing a clearinghouse of web 2.0 applications (www.curriculum21.com /clearinghouse). Searching educational websites, we found a kind of *"edu-kitchen sink"* that contained everything from quasi-mathematics games in the same vein as *Angry Birds* to traditional, short, self-directed flash cards like Quizlet and vocabulary builders like Visuwords. What we encountered certainly validated the complaints and concerns of the educators asking the question, "Where do I dive into this mélange of apps?"

We began by creating *tags*. As the word suggests, tags are labels that set up categories for organizational and search purposes. We then began our first round of tagging. Although it was a good place to start, it quickly became clear that many if not most of the applications and tools were interdisciplinary in nature. So we cross-tagged, which was very helpful for teachers. For example, the Google Art Project (www.google.com/culturalinstitute/project/art-project), which takes the user to art collections all over the world, is tagged not only as art but also as history and social studies. Then new angles on types of tags emerged. We decided to add age groups, and in some instances it seemed to help, but it, too, proved more complex. For example, I initially tagged ZooBurst (www.zooburst.com), which allows the user to create three-dimensional pop-up books, as *early childhood*. Then, I began to view the ZooBurst gallery of samples, which was filled with high school student work, as well as work from world language classes from a range of students. Thus, one of the key findings of our tagging was that, unlike the literal and concrete limitations of a school library, where you have one copy of a book that can only go in one place, the marvelous array of web 2.0 applications begs for multiple locations, and these locations are fluid.

Teachers can model for students the analytic skill of strategically cross-tagging applications. However, before doing this in the classroom, a teacher or group of teachers might begin by tagging applications in specific categories or types from specific content areas, types of sources, or purposes. For example, a category tag might be Math, Communication, or Media Making. Students can see that some of the applications belong in several tags. Besides receiving feedback on the sorting process, working through the initial tagging experience with colleagues is a great way to gather and share more resources. Ultimately, the goal is to encourage our students to slow down in order to deliberately review, categorize, and vet applications and website resources available to them. Identifying the function and quality of a site enables teachers and students to match it to specific units of study and classroom activities in a clearinghouse, as described in the fifth action step (see page 33).

Following are lists of applications and websites that can help cultivate sophistication on the part of the learner.

Networking applications:

- Twitter (www.twitter.com) is a popular social media tool for following individuals and groups and cultivating a following on any subject or topic.

- Blogster (www.blogster.com) is a basic platform for establishing public or privately shared blog commentary with groups.

- Edmodo (www.edmodo.com) is one of the most secure sites for sharing posts, assignments, and communication between teachers and students.

- Wikispaces (www.wikispaces.com) is a platform for setting up a common webpage for any group for any purpose.

Broadcasting applications:

- Skype (www.skype.com) allows for both video conferencing and audio conferencing worldwide.

- Google Hangouts (www.google.com/hangouts) supports video and audio conferencing among ten locations simultaneously.

- WebEx (www.webex.com), InstantPresenter (www.instantpresenter.com), and Adobe Connect (www.adobe.com/products/adobeconnect.html) are webinar platforms that support presentations between a presenter and locations worldwide with interaction from the audience via chat and icon responses. Slides, images, screensharing, and live camera images of the presenter are available.

- Podbean (www.podbean.com) is a free service that enables a school to have its own podcasting channel.

Repository information sources:

- National Geographic EarthPulse (www.nationalgeographic.com/earth pulse/population.html) provides striking visual and moving images on information regarding the human condition and our relationship to the environment.

- New York Public Library's Biblion (http://exhibitions.nypl.org/biblion) provides in-depth visual material, primary source documents, and articles, such as those on the 1939–1940 New York World's Fair (http://exhibitions.nypl.org/biblion/worldsfair).

- Library of Congress (www.loc.gov) is the world's largest library.

Computational and statistical resources:

- WolframAlpha (www.wolframalpha.com) makes computation come alive with opportunities to collect and to calculate statistics in all subjects in a dynamic sequence of steps.

- The National Library of Virtual Manipulatives (http://nlvm.usu.edu) offers sets of virtual manipulatives based on grade spans (preK–2, 3–5, 6–8, and 9–12) and mathematics concepts: number and operations, algebra, measurement, geometry, data analysis, and probability.

- Worldmapper (www.worldmapper.org) visualizes data about categories of demographic information regarding global patterns and distorts images to match the statistic per country.

- Poodwaddle World Clock (www.poodwaddle.com/clocks/worldclock) keeps track moment to moment on global statistics like births, deaths, and debt.

Composition for writing:

- VoiceThread (http://voicethread.com) is a multimedia slideshow tool for groups to share and build stories and commentary.

- Storybird (http://storybird.com) is a story-creation tool that supports short, art-inspired stories you can make and share on any device.

- ZooBurst (www.zooburst.com) supports the design and writing of 3-D pop-up books.

- Famous Inboxes (www.famousinboxes.com) uses examples to prompt students to write their own versions of clever and creative fantasy inboxes of famous people in history, celebrities, and characters in fiction.

- Plotblot (www.plotbot.com) is a screenplay-writing tool that reflects the standard form for scripts and allows for collaborative work.

Location and travel:

- Google Maps (https://maps.google.com) supports location and directions from any spot on the planet using both standard and satellite images.

- HERE (http://here.com/traffic) provides real-time data about traffic patterns across the world.

- KAYAK (www.kayak.com) supports flight information point-to-point for locations worldwide.

When designing a tagging activity for students, the key is to ask them not only to sort according to given criteria but also to eventually develop their own categories. Tagging is a way to operationalize analysis and synthesis. Tagging is reflected in the Common Core ELA Reading Anchor Standards for Informational Text, which involves determining the relationship between craft and structure (NGA & CCSSO, 2010). How do we structure and organize informational sources that students craft in a digital web 2.0 format?

Curate a Classroom Clearinghouse to Organize and Match Tags to Units and Courses

A hiker on a trek feels a particular joy when encountering a clearing that beckons him or her to stop, sit, and reflect. In this same spirit, we should invite our learners to stop with us to consider what resources and tools best support a curricular journey. Meaningful curricular choices will be made more frequently in a joint effort between teacher and learner to review and share digital media resources. A clearinghouse for digital tools, networking sites, and applications is a virtual outcome and a major performance task. Shaping the layout, accessibility, and navigation of the clearinghouse is under the bailiwick of *curation* skills, which has been defined as "maintaining, preserving, and adding value to digital research data through its lifecycle" (Digital Curation Centre, 2012).

An outgrowth of digital curation and maintenance for our purposes is that teachers collaborate with learners using a virtual presence on a website and create a class clearinghouse. In this process, students and teachers can go deeper into their curriculum units and employ tagging to create a resource bank of purposeful, interactive web 2.0 applications and repository sites from which to draw. Through direct and clear instruction, teachers can walk through the process of submitting a site or application with the annotation directed to one or more tags on a unit-specific clearinghouse. Prior to their submissions, students and teachers can review helpful and clear annotations with summary descriptions as examples. (To find entries in the Curriculum 21 Clearinghouse, visit www.curriculum21 .com/clearinghouse.) The clearinghouse turns a simple resource list into a targeted, hyperlinked, sophisticated site. For example, a science teacher can click on the clearinghouse tab and move his cursor to SHOW–ALL RESOURCES, which results in a pop-up window of over thirty tags. He or she moves the cursor to SCIENCE, which in turn opens to pages of featured entries. The teacher scrolls down the page and selects Interactive Solar System (www.solarsystem scope.com) to employ in the astronomy unit. What emerges is that the actual design and curation of the clearinghouse becomes a formative assessment task. In another example, Ms. Parker's fifth-grade class webpage (visit **go.solution-tree .com/21stcenturyskills**) is attractive, engaging, and easy to navigate, and her elementary students can click through the resources tied to their current units of study.

Creating a clearinghouse allows students to provide evidence of operational digital literacy, including the ability to identify sources; analyze, set, and apply criteria, and organize content. The next step would be to ask each student to create a personal clearinghouse posted on his or her personal webpage.

Create a Digital Design Solution Project as a Graduation Requirement

What makes a graduation diploma meaningful for the future? Can a graduation requirement motivate students toward excellence and productivity? It is time to rethink and replace some dated graduation goals. What type of major assessment task would reflect a high level of literacy and a student's ability to employ digital tools? A dynamic alternative to graduation requirements would be the creation of a digitally designed project that solves a real-world problem. The impetus for engagement in the real world is not new; it has been ingrained in our collective pedagogy since John Dewey (1938; 1998) first began to focus on experiential learning. The Common Core State Standards have been explicit in declaring that their goal is to prepare students to be career and college ready for the future.

The merging of project-based learning (PBL) with contemporary technologies provides a viable approach to rethinking graduation products and performances. The Buck Institute for Education (www.bie.org) is providing detailed guidance on how to implement PBL. The institute provides "a systematic teaching method which engages students in learning important knowledge and 21st century skills through an extended, student-influenced inquiry process" (Buck Institute for Education, 2011, p. 5). The inquiry process is based on rigorous consideration of meaningful content to identify a problem and generate something new as a product. Collaboration, review, and communication are central to the process. The projects are intended to be powerful and demanding, with constant review and monitoring from peers, teachers, and the larger community.

A marvelous set of examples of how high schools can adopt PBL can be found at Gary and Jerri-Ann Jacobs High Tech High in San Diego, which is one of a group of eleven internationally recognized trail-blazing K–12 schools. High Tech High's forte is a creative focus on rigorous productivity using modern digital media. There are teacher-designed projects directly related to curriculum, ranging from a blood-bank project to a not-for-profit deliverables project. What is particularly impressive is that the projects emerge from the full range of academic courses, rather than strictly from the technology teacher. The school site (www.hightechhigh.org/schools/HTH) offers examples of student digital portfolios reflecting the individual quests of learners required for graduation. Given the motivation and quality of the projects that emerge, moving more schools in North America to take action on making a long-term PBL a requisite rather than an enrichment activity makes sense.

The amalgamation of problem-solving strategies, marketing consideration, technical planning, real-world testing, and timely innovation is crystallized in the design of a successful app. The term *app* has become ubiquitous as our use of and dependency on these useful tools have become integrated into our lives, whether it is using Google Maps to determine traffic patterns, Team Stream to follow your favorite team's scores, POLITICO to follow your least favorite politician, Reading Friends: Jungle A to Z to enable your five-year-old to practice the alphabet, or Skywatcher to dazzle your friends with a look at the night (or daytime) sky and locate a constellation. Imagine if your students were engaged in app design as a graduation requirement.

Getting started requires a critique of existing apps by students to consider what qualities make them popular and useful. Students go on to brainstorm and propose possibilities. In her article in *Smashing Magazine*, "How to Create Your First iPhone App (2012 Edition)," Jen Gordon (2012) provides potential app designers with start-up questions and resources: "What is your goal?" "What are your expectations?" "Where do I begin?" She proceeds to detail practical considerations unique to app design. Students would be well advised to read the point of view of professionals like Gordon in order to understand more about the worlds of marketing, finance, and design.

Extensive programming or coding skills are not necessary in the entry phase of app design. At Winchester High School in Winchester, Massachusetts, teacher Daniel Downs has developed the course Designing Apps for Androids in which students propose, critique, design, test, and share applications. In the first two months of the course, Mr. Down's students released thirty-two apps for children (Marra, 2011)!

The school that wishes to start at a more modest level can download free software programs, such as GameSalad, that provide a visual development environment to help students learn about the basics of editing, graphics, and design. In this instance, a technology specialist can work with subject-area teachers or students to create an app.

Students can submit their app for widespread use in the general population through a mobile company or software platform, and many of the app-making tools do not require programming skills. Teachers can direct and coach students toward the ultimate real-world solution using the following resources.

- Mobile App Maker by Conduit (http://mobile.conduit.com)
- Windows Phone AppStudio by Microsoft (http://apps.windowsstore.com)
- Apple Developer (https://developer.apple.com)
- Android Developers (http://developer.android.com/guide/components/index.html)

- Overview: Facebook Developers (https://developers.facebook.com/docs/guides/canvas)
- AppDesigner (www.appdesigner.com)
- Google Apps Platform (https://developers.google.com/google-apps)

Designing an app is one example of how creating a digital solution could prove to be an engaging interdisciplinary graduation task. The activities involved in layout, sequencing, aesthetics, business, marketing, and communicating the outcome allow students to develop genuine career and college readiness.

Conclusion

In the second decade of the 21st century, the majority of classrooms consists of four walls and open portals to virtual learning. Thirty years from the writing of this book, the classroom will look very different. Maybe there will no longer be class*rooms*. Perhaps there will be a range of learning spaces—both physical and virtual—in which students create and share their work. Any educator reading these words is a central figure in making the transition to a modern learning environment. Whatever physical form new classrooms take, educators will still need to make curricular choices. The contemporary teacher and administrator can choose to help students access digital tools, determine what makes an effective selection, organize those tools through tagging, create a clearinghouse to match a curricular purpose, and design an app as a contribution toward solving a problem.

References and Resources

Bejar, I. I. (2010). Can speech technology improve assessment and learning? New capabilities may facilitate assessment innovations. *R&D Connections, 15*, 1–8.

Broadband Data Improvement Act of 2008, 47 U.S.C. § 254 (2008).

Buck Institute for Education. (2011). *PBL in the elementary grades*. Novato, CA: Author.

Dewey, J. (1938). *Experience and education*. West Lafayette, IN: Kappa Delta Pi.

Dewey, J. (1998). *Experience and education* (60th anniversary ed.). West Lafayette, IN: Kappa Delta Pi.

Digital Curation Centre. (2013). *What is digital curation?* Accessed at www.dcc.ac.uk/digital-curation/what-digital-curation on October 28, 2012.

Ellcessor, L. (2009, May 28). People I want to know: Twitter, celebrity, and social connection. *Flow, 9*(14). Accessed at http://flowtv.org/2009/05/people-i-want-to

-know-twitter-celebrity-and-social-connectionliz-ellcessor-university-of-wisconsin
-madison on April 1, 2013.

Gordon, J. (2012, January 10). *How to create your first iPhone app (2012 edition).*
Accessed at http://mobile.smashingmagazine.com/2009/08/11/how-to-create
-your-first-iphone-application on April 10, 2013.

Hegarty, B., Penman, M., Kelly, O., Jeffrey, L., Coburn, D., & McDonald, J.
(2010). *Digital information literacy: Supported development of capability in tertiary
environments—Final report.* Dunedin, New Zealand: Otago Polytechnic.
Accessed at www.educationcounts.govt.nz/publications/tertiary_education/80624
on April 1, 2013.

Hertz, M. B. (2012, June 4). How to teach Internet safety to younger elementary
students [Web log post]. Accessed at www.edutopia.org/blog/internet-safety
-younger-elementary-mary-beth-hertz on October 26, 2012.

Hinduja, S., & Patchin, J. W. (2013). *State cyberbullying laws: A brief review of state
cyberbullying laws and policies.* Eau Clair, WI: Cyberbullying Research Center.
Accessed at www.cyberbullying.us/Bullying_and_Cyberbullying_Laws.pdf on
November 14, 2013.

Information and Communications Technology Council. (2010). *Digital literacy:
Canada's productivity opportunity* [White paper]. Ottawa, Ontario, Canada: Author.

International Society for Technology in Education. (2007). *National Educational
Technology Standards for Students* (2nd ed.). Washington, DC: Author.

i-SAFE. (2013). *School safety = i-SAFE: The i-SAFE Foundation.* Accessed at http://
isafe.org/wp/?page_id=211 on May 17, 2013.

Jacobs, H. H. (Ed.). (2010). *Curriculum 21: Essential education for a changing world.*
Alexandria, VA: Association for Supervision and Curriculum Development.

Jones-Kavalier, B. R., & Flannigan, S. L. (2006). Connecting the digital dots: Literacy
of the 21st century. *EDUCAUSE Quarterly.* Accessed at www.educause.edu/ero
/article/connecting-digital-dots-literacy-21st-century on August 8, 2013.

Kirk, M. (2013, January 11). iPads a success at Caston. *Pharos-Tribune.* Accessed
at http://pharostribune.com/local/x503818838/iPads-a-success-at-Caston on
November 14, 2013.

Marra, D. (2011, November 27). Winchester High School's new course: "Designing
applications (apps) for Androids"—Winchester High School class takes advantage
of technology. *Winchester Patch.* Accessed at http://winchester.patch.com/groups
/schools/p/winchester-high-school-s-new-course-designing-applica194a5c1148 on
August 8, 2013.

McArthur, J. A. (2011, November 18). *Voicing a Campus Icon: Twitter, a bronze goddess, and hyperlocal community engagement* [Video file]. Accessed at www.jamcarthur.com on November 12, 2013.

Metz, R. (2012). Tablet makers pursue public schools: High schools, grammar schools, and kindergartens are a large and growing market for Apple's iPad. *MIT Technology Review.* Accessed at www.technologyreview.com/news/506321/tablet-makers-pursue-public-schools on April 10, 2013.

Mitchell, K. (2013, January 11). iPads a success at Caston: Devices create efficiency and enhance learning. *Pharos-Tribune.* Accessed at http://pharostribune.com/local/x503818838/iPads-a-success-at-Caston on May 17, 2013.

National Center for Technology Innovation. (2010). *Speech recognition for learning.* Accessed at www.ldonline.org/article/Speech_Recognition_for_Learning?theme=print on May 17, 2013.

National Conference of State Legislatures. (2012, February 15). *Children and the Internet: Laws relating to filtering, blocking and usage policies in schools and libraries.* Accessed at www.ncsl.org/issues-research/telecom/state-internet-filtering-laws.aspx#states on October 27, 2012.

National Cyber Security Alliance. (2011). *The state of K–12 cyberethics, cybersafety and cybersecurity curriculum in the United States.* Accessed at staysafeonline.org/download/datasets/2052/2011_national_k12_study.pdf#sthash.L33Yytru.dpuf on October 26, 2012.

National Governors Association Center for Best Practices & Council of Chief State School Officers. (2010). *Common Core State Standards for English language arts and literacy in history/social science, science, & technical subjects.* Washington, DC: Authors. Accessed at www.corestandards.org/assets/CCSSI_ELA%20Standards.pdf on August 15, 2013.

Purcell, K., Rainie, L., Heaps, A., Buchanan J., Friedrich, L., Jacklin, A., et al. (2012). *How teens do research in the digital world.* Washington, DC: Pew Internet & American Life Project. Accessed at http://pewinternet.org/Reports/2012/Student-Research on November 8, 2012.

State of New South Wales Curriculum Learning Innovation Centre. (2012). *Use of tablet technology in the classroom.* Strathfield, New South Wales, Australia: State of New South Wales Department of Education and Communities. Accessed at www.tale.edu.au/tale/live/teachers/shared/next_practice/iPad_Evaluation_Sydney_Region.pdf on June 5, 2013.

TechTerms.com. (2012). *App.* Accessed at www.techterms.com/definition/app on May 17, 2013.

Thompson, C. (2013). *Smarter than your think: How technology is changing our minds for the better.* New York: Penguin.

Trubek, A. (2011, August 15). Out of touch with typing. *MIT Technology Review.* Accessed at www.technologyreview.com/view/425018/out-of-touch-with-typing on November 14, 2013.

Steve Hargadon is the director of Web 2.0 Labs and host of the Future of Education interview series. He is the creator and organizer of a collection of worldwide virtual conferences that include the annual Global Education Conference and Library 2.0 Future of Libraries conference, which help to build community, connections, and learning opportunities for teachers, students, administrators, and families. His networks and events draw over one hundred thousand participants annually.

Steve pioneered the use of social networking in education by creating the Classroom 2.0 social network in 2007, and he has supported and encouraged the development of thousands of other education networks, particularly for professional development. He is the cohost of the annual Edublog Awards, was the former emerging technologies chair for the International Society for Technology in Education, and was the recipient of the Computer-Using Educators' 2010 Technology in Learning Leadership Award. He has consulted for PBS, Intel, Ning, Blackboard, Microsoft, KnowledgeWorks Foundation, CoSN, MERLOT, the U.S. Department of State, the U.S. Department of Education, and other organizations and institutions on educational technology and specifically on social networking.

Visit www.stevehargadon.com to learn more about Steve's work.

To book Steve Hargadon for professional development, contact pd@solution-tree.com.

Chapter 3

Notes From the Revolution: Peer-Driven Social Learning Communities

By Steve Hargadon

There is no questioning it: a revolution is taking place. In March of 2008, I wrote an article with the bold title "Web 2.0 Is the Future of Education" (Hargadon, 2008), and aside from the hubris that surely drove such a declaration, there was the practical sense that the tools of web 2.0 did promise tangible opportunities for classroom and learning engagement. Even so, I'm not sure that we realized the dramatic reshaping about to take place in our perceptions of learning or the building of learning opportunities that would occur because of social media.

Social Learning

In many ways, social media—the use of the web as a means of interaction between or among people—has not just opened new doors to creativity and collaboration: it has also refocused the collective attention of educators to the importance of engagement, initiative, creation, and participation as significant parts of the learning experience.

In the spring of 2010, I gave a series of presentations in France, including one to secondary-aged students. I asked them to list the websites they used most frequently and then to identify those that were educational. They included several popular sites, like YouTube, high on their list, but they did not consider these sites to be educational. Given the fairly amazing amount of informal teaching and learning that YouTube, for example, allows, I asked why they didn't consider their use of YouTube to be educational. Their response haunts me: "Because we're not taking notes." For them, learning was only learning if it involved taking notes.

Watching someone on YouTube play a song on the guitar, then uploading your own version of the same song, or even just watching and comparing some of the hundreds or thousands of versions of a new viral video trend, at the very least involves some passive learning and often what we would call very active learning activities. Social media is reminding us in huge ways that learning does in fact take place outside of formal institutions where it often is a highly social experience.

I don't think this is a big surprise. Consider the experiences we have at formal conferences. There, relatively passive learning comes from watching prepared presentations, but a more active and social form of learning happens in the hallways and over meals with other participants and presenters, where we share, challenge, and build on ideas. I will often ask audiences in my presentations to remember their deepest learning experiences and then to share the experiences and the conditions that led to them. Those experiences are less frequently in what we would call formal learning settings. More often, they have a high degree of hands-on involvement or are related to very memorable and personal moments when someone else—often a teacher—expressed personal confidence in them, challenged them, or believed in them when they didn't believe in themselves.

As the web is helping us remember the importance of the social aspects of learning, we are also becoming aware of the degree to which memorization and rote learning have triumphed in an age-old battle between learning imposed on the student and learning constructed *by* the student. Like the students in France, when we regard learning as a passive or solo activity, we constrain our cultural perspectives on where, how, and with whom learning actually takes place.

It has been fascinating for me to see how involvement in social media can radically shift perspectives on learning. I often hear those who have become or are becoming involved in social media for education use dramatic language to describe a change in their own learning and in their beliefs about learning. In my own case, I frequently relate how participating online through blogging and podcasting spurred within me a "personal cognitive revolution," marking one of the most important transitions in my life—from that of a consumer of information to an active participant in building knowledge with others. I can tell you about the first time I participated in a dialogue on the web, and I have vivid and even emotional memories of many of my first interactions as an online participant. That it felt foreign to me—someone who loved learning and reading—to be proactive or to participate, is a telling measure of the degree to which my own conceptions of learning were largely based in passivity.

Learning Spaces

Because I am not the only one who had this experience on the web, educators and others have been asking important questions about how we construct learning spaces. When we accepted the primacy of top-down learning as our education paradigm, we of course mirrored that belief in the construction of our learning spaces. We conceived and built them to facilitate the transmission of knowledge in a hierarchical manner. When we see learning as having much broader, flatter, and more social components, we start to ask new questions about what learning spaces look like and how they are constructed. Of huge significance is our acceptance of the social nature of learning, which alters not just our beliefs about what learning spaces look like and how they are constructed but also *who constructs them*.

Mirrored Learning Worlds

Because I have been both a consumer and producer of web-based learning spaces, in the balance of this chapter I hope to share some practical lessons about social learning spaces and the models of learning they reflect. As well, our discussion of social learning will also illuminate the ways in which the learning worlds that teachers and students inhabit are mirrored.

In traditional top-down education, the learning worlds of the teachers and students are equally rigid, one-way experiences. In socially-constructed learning, both teachers and students build flexible and highly personal learning spaces, and familiarity with this building process is critical in order for teachers to guide students through it. In the building of learning spaces, our ultimate goal transcends the acquisition of facts and figures—our goal is instead the creation of framework structures for ourselves that promote long-term growth in social learning and self-directed ways.

Without an understanding of how this building process takes place, the teacher cannot be helpful to the student in this world of socially constructed learning the web has so significantly enabled. Helping learners to participate in this new learning world, then, starts with focusing on an understanding of how educators—adults who are focused on learning—can do the very same thing. Thinking of teachers primarily as learners, and giving them opportunities to learn in social learning spaces provides them the opportunity to reinvigorate (and often rediscover) their own learning, thereby being able to help their students access the same methods, and, perhaps most importantly, to model learning to both students and colleagues.

In the broader context, the social and intellectual growth that comes from peer learning is not as easy to measure as the test-taking methods of rote learning, but its greater significance to both the learner and society require that we reshape ideas and policies around more authentic, learner-driven opportunities. Ideas and activities do not live in isolation; they are constructed and shaped within social contexts. Writing, videomaking, and other forms of creation, contribution, and feedback around real-world ideas are vital for helping learners explore passions and skills in ways that will make a difference to their communities and the world.

I'm also convinced from my own experiences and those of others that increasing our abilities to create and be self-directed leads to emotional fulfillment, and that educators are more likely to realize the joys of teaching through opportunities to engage with peers.

Democratized Learning Spaces

It is critically important to see that the learning worlds of teachers and students are mirrored as we watch technological trends increasingly allow for the easy, and often free, building of social learning communities. Sal Khan creates a set of recorded videos for his nephews, and a huge learning community comes into being in Khan Academy (www.khanacademy.org). I create a social network for educators called Classroom 2.0 (www.classroom20.com), and 75,000 educators join in the discussion. Someone interested in gardening or guitar playing or lacrosse uploads some videos to YouTube and a community of followers often forms, even if it's only three people.

In a hierarchical learning world, there can be both large perceived and real differences in learning opportunities between a community of millions, a community of thousands, or a group of three. On the web, group size no longer equates to organizational capability or access to resources. This shift away from size determining opportunity, when added to the power and importance of learning from peers, has significant consequences as it greatly enlarges the boundaries, breadth, and depth of learning opportunities; and technology has been very much at the heart of this change.

In early 2007, Ning, the commercial (and at that time free-of-charge) platform for social web development started by Marc Andreessen and Gina Bianchini, pivoted its business model to be a "build your own social network" service by springboarding off the popularity of Myspace and Facebook. This shift allowed educators and others to build thousands of educational social networks around their teaching subjects and personal interests, and it is currently being expanded by the new Google+ communities, which will allow anyone to build an online social community around any topic in a fraction of the time and at no cost.

Online community technologies did not start with Ning, as those familiar with electronic mail lists, the WELL, or Tapped In might know. However, the ease of use that came from the intuitive, graphical, and browser-based spaces of Myspace and Facebook, when married by Ning to the ability of anyone to create such spaces, was a quantum leap in organizational capacity and topic specialization. My Classroom 2.0 site, built on the Ning platform, was essentially a "Myspace" for educators interested in the use of web 2.0 technologies in the classroom. As social networking technology became much more accessible, and the potential for creation became much greater, the building of online learning spaces for learning turned into a massive opportunity for participation. By focusing on stand-alone communities and specifically encouraging educators to create them, Ning has played a critical role in the democratization of social learning spaces on the web.

Google+ communities, which at the time of this writing do not have the same robustness as Ning networks, are continuing this trend of democratizing community creation. While the particular fortunes of companies providing these services may wax and wane, along with their popularity, a Pandora's box has been opened. The positive empowerment for building learning spaces and communities has been unleashed and cannot be retracted.

Online Events

Another important democratizing trend we see is from synchronous virtual online meeting platforms like Blackboard Collaborate, WebEx, GoToMeeting, Adobe Connect, Skype, and Google Hangouts. While the technologies will obviously continue to change and improve, the message is clear: anyone can build a learning space anywhere, anytime, and (currently), for free with some of the tools.

As I write this chapter, I am at a small school for the children of leprosy-affected adults in rural India. Yesterday, I watched the schoolchildren perform a choreographed dance version of a South Korean pop song, which after an hour of relatively boring speakers, sent the kids into explosive clapping and cheering (much to the chagrin of their teachers). My wife and several others took videos of this moment, which they have probably already shared through Facebook or YouTube. This morning, I woke up early, and over a 13.5 hour time difference, did a video-based interview with the author of a book on parenting and education, which dozens of people from around the world watched live, and which others will watch as a recorded version.

To claim that these synchronous and near-synchronous technologies will dramatically impact learning does not feel like hyperbole. In fact, it feels like such a moment of importance that it creates a moral imperative to help these students, who face no small amount of discrimination because of their parents' disease, to become more knowledgeable about building their own learning spaces.

The Nitty-Gritty

To explore the lessons that social learning spaces hold for formal discussions of learning and learning theory, I'm going to share some very practical experiences from my years of creating and tending online communities and events.

In an interesting shift in influence, a number of offline or physical events have been enhanced because of the accessibility of online spaces for real-time organizing and record-keeping, where participants create these user-generated meetings in real time. The meetings go by a variety of names—such as *unconferences* or *barcamps*—and they typically start with a blank slate at the beginning of the day, with attendees creating and scheduling sessions on topics that they want to discuss. My experiences with organizing synchronous online events and user-generated physical events will also be part of the background framework as I propose a set of lessons for those wanting to build or facilitate social learning spaces.

First, let me give some historical context.

A Little History

I first learned about educational blogging in 2005–2006, while speaking at conferences focused on the educational uses of technology, where I presented on the opportunities to use open-source software in schools. As I learned about how blogging was being used in education, I began to see glimmers of the tremendous value that could come from teachers connecting with other teachers directly on the web. However, the promise that blogging held of the ability to share practices and reduce isolation had three significant hurdles. The first was a fairly steep learning curve, mostly around setting up a server or software for the blogging. The second was that the new blogger can count on many months of blogging to the empty room—that is, writing with no audience until others happen to find him or her.

The final hurdle may have been the highest—blogging carried the expectation of "completed" writing. Whether by virtue of its being based on the traditional blank page or because of cultural expectations, a blog post was expected to be long-form writing. The work involved in blogging therefore turned out to be fairly intimidating to most educators, since they were also quite used to the criticism that accompanies that form. After all, teachers were familiar with the experience of criticizing the writing of students. As well, it can be hard for a teacher to be comfortable with anything other than the traditional expectations of writing for an audience.

With the hours or days it might take to figure out how to choose a blogging service (usually at a cost in those early days), the technical requirements of actually setting up the blog, and of course the requirement that you have something important enough to say, it's easy to see how daunting blogging had been and still is to educators, especially as it seemed one blogging mistake could haunt you forever. (This was largely the legacy of print media, in which very little content made it to the printed page and whatever did was expected to have no glaring errors, either grammatical or logical.)

It's no small wonder that even with the promises of personal fulfillment and growth that conference speakers were giving, only a very small minority of educators were actually blogging. In 2006, I held a gathering of educational bloggers prior to the National Educational Computing Conference (now the International Society for Technology in Education [ISTE]); over one hundred attended, and it was our best guess as a group that over half of the then-known educational bloggers were present. (This event continues to this day on the day before ISTE—see www.isteunplugged.com.)

Introducing Classroom 2.0

In this environment of low adoption, but with an awareness of the value of blogging even with these high hurdles to overcome, I interviewed the cofounders of Ning for my podcast series (the soon to be titled "The Future of Education"— www.futureofeducation.com), and I started to keep track of their project. In early 2007, Ning shifted its model from being primarily an open platform for web development to a service where users could easily build their own social networks. It was quickly evident to me that something really important had just happened, and in March 2007, Classroom 2.0, a Ning network for educators to talk to each other about social media as a classroom tool, was born.

For educators, social networking had some immediate benefits over blogging. First, when you became a member, you didn't have to wait months to find others or for them to find you. Given that we believed there were fewer than two hundred educators blogging at the time, when we reached five hundred members in Classroom 2.0 there was a tremendous rush of excitement. Some of the better-known educational bloggers would come into Classroom 2.0 and be shocked at how many people were there whom they didn't know and had never seen contributing on the web. "That's the idea!" I would say. Those who had been trudging up the bloggin' hill all by themselves, earning their reputations by perseverance and patience, were a tad resentful of these upstart shortcutters. "It'll never fly" was a pretty common sentiment. (Translation: "It *should* never fly.")

But Classroom 2.0 survived and grew. Not only did our Ning network provide an immediate set of people to connect to (*friending* became a legitimate verb, now a form of connecting with colleagues), but the form of legitimate posts changed. With so many participants so immediately able to respond, and with a format of threaded discussion, five-paragraph essays quickly gave way to thoughts condensed to a sentence or two—or just a query, observation, or discussion starter. As the formal gave way to the informal, and as short contributions could be more confidently spell- and grammar-checked (several times, I'm sure, for most first-time posters), fear gave way to the exhilaration of making immediate connections and receiving what seemed like immediate responses from peers.

So, it came about that Classroom 2.0 burgeoned beyond our wildest expectations, and I soon started doing consulting work for Ning, evangelizing their platform for education. As educators and learners found topics that they wanted to discuss outside of social media in education, network after network spun out of Classroom 2.0. Soon individuals created hundreds and then thousands of other free Ning networks as learning spaces to cultivate, curate, and oversee.

Just as Myspace and Facebook ushered in new eras of participation because of their combination of visual and social features, so too did Ning, but with the added benefit of topic specialization and, importantly, broad proactive participation from creators. While Facebook and Twitter have undoubtedly brought larger numbers of educators to social media, Ning paved the way for distributed leadership in building learning spaces.

Building Synchronous Online Events

It was in the context and through the growth of Classroom 2.0 that I began to hold live, virtual events with educators using Elluminate, an online tool for live virtual classroom teaching. In 2010, Lucy Gray and I started the Global Education Conference (http://globaleducationconference.com), a free, five-day, twenty-four-hour virtual event to gather educators worldwide to share with each other how they were connecting students and classrooms from different cultures and countries. The conference has since spawned several other worldwide virtual conferences, including the Library 2.0 Future of Libraries conference and the new School Leadership Summit (see all of them at www.web20labs.com).

The virtual conference represents, I believe, another significant shift in thinking about learning spaces. While many organizations are replicating their physical conferences online, the Global Education Conference and the other Web 2.0

Labs conferences demonstrate that virtual conferences, freed from the traditional constraints of time, travel, and physical space, can and should shift their focus from being highly and often subjectively selective events to something much more akin to social networking. These venues should allow anyone who wants to, and is reasonably addressing the topic at hand, to present. By becoming highly inclusive, we dramatically reduce the overhead of vetting committees, as well as the often-made accusations of preferential treatment to certain speakers. Surprisingly to us as organizers (at first, but not anymore), we have found that even with an open participation framework the quality of presentations has stayed quite high.

The benefit of this model to individual educators in terms of their own personal and intellectual growth is hard to overstate. When the audience can decide what sessions to attend, we don't have to reduce the number of those who can present. A presentation can be viable with only a few attendees, and all sessions can be recorded for later viewing. Regardless of the size of the audience, many presenters are thrilled to share their ideas and grow professionally, and the opportunity to share with colleagues is a milestone in their careers.

Holding Unconferences

Soon after the start of Classroom 2.0, in addition to running the annual EduBloggerCon at ISTE and a few other educational technology conferences, I started a series of city-by-city events called the Classroom 2.0 Workshops. These unconferences were also free events, because we had an early and generous set of sponsors. We held them throughout the United States, using wikis for organizing. A wiki, as Adam Frey of Wikispaces would often tell me, is just a webpage with an edit button. With their ability to have multiple editors, wikis opened the door to collaboratively designed events. I would create the hour-by-hour framework for the day, and educators local to the physical venue would add topics or sessions. Fans of these kinds of events have since created additional offerings, such as the current Edcamp program (http://edcamp.wikispaces.com), that go well beyond these early endeavors.

Lessons Learned

As just described, I have been privileged to participate in three different forms of activity that reflect, and hopefully have helped to expand, opportunities for peer-driven social learning for educators. During this time, several specific themes have emerged. These themes and the conclusions I draw from them are different, I submit, from much of the community-building advice given for institutionally created communities, as the paradigm for governance of peer-created communities differs somewhat from that of formal educational institutions. With tens of millions of educators worldwide whose areas of expertise and interest are broad and wide, practitioners themselves are creating most of the social learning spaces. Their responsibilities and motivations are likely to be independent of the organizations they work for, and this independence will lead to the need and the opportunity for them to create their own paradigms for building virtual learning communities.

Where an institution is likely to measure success through traditional metrics—numbers of members or quantified equations of participation and engagement—the individual starting a community around a passion or personal interest may never track those numbers very closely. Instead, he or she will care more deeply about the connections people make, the opportunities available from such engagement, and the personal fulfillment that comes from collaboration on a specific topic or ideas. The following lessons are not likely to be exhaustive, but they should serve as an opportunity to build a helpful conversation. (Visit www .stevehargadon.com for follow-up conversations.)

1. **It starts (and finishes) with the members.** One of the first lessons of social communities is that they truly distribute the wisdom of the network, and the unique experiences of diverse networks make social learning communities leveraging this wisdom more likely to survive and thrive.

2. **It's not about you. It's about the users.** Web 2.0 is about participation, and the first and maybe most important lesson of creating a web 2.0 network or service is encouraging others and providing an environment for them in which to participate and even to lead. Instead of managing for an outcome, we are managing for a process of engagement, and that means caring first about the users and being aware that by helping them you will ultimately gain the best reward you can hope for as a creator: participants' authentic, true growth.

3. **The early adopters influence the community and its usefulness even more than the creator.** Early adopters are the ones most likely to tell others about the community or conversations, and they will be the ones who will recognize what you can do to provide the most relevant platform. This has been most publicly recognizable with Twitter, where the use of the network and some of the most important innovations have come from the users.

4. **Web 2.0 depends on user-generated content.** If you build a learning space or network that is not dependent on and supportive of the excitement, active participation, and even leadership of your members, it may be a sign you're trying to overlay web 2.0 on a top-down traditional

model. You can't provide only for collaborative content; you also have to provide for collaborative *building*. In a world with so many ways people can spend their time, you have to provide an opportunity for those important early adopters to take part in determining where the network goes and how people use it. Early adopters are also often attracted to places where they can play roles of significance that bring them visibility and opportunity, and so you have to help them get that. If you don't provide an environment where others can function and be seen as leaders, they will go somewhere they can.

5. **Members are building their own online reputations or brands and appreciate being recognized.** The more you can authentically compliment, thank, acknowledge, and showcase the work of others, the more likely your members will feel rewarded for their participation. As other members see your generosity, they will be encouraged to contribute. There is an implied and fair contract with community members that they will trade their valuable time building a social community if they are recognized for their work. It is not egotistical for members to expect and appreciate attention; it's a fair recognition of their value.

6. **Volunteerism is the lifeblood of a peer social community.** It should be a warning sign if you or someone else responsible for your learning space considers paying others for their participation. Your association with other learners should be akin to how you would treat someone in a church community, the Red Cross, or a fraternal association.

7. **Grassroots projects, with varying degrees of oversight, are now creating outcomes that we have normally associated with top-level control.** The power shift that I mentioned at the beginning of this chapter is very real, and it is leading to deinstitutionalization in many areas, including education, that have depended on institutional structures for governance. The difficulty this creates for us is that we have a hard time overcoming our previous expectation about how things get built. An obvious, but no less invaluable, example is Wikipedia (www.wikipedia.org). As an encyclopedia distributed through widespread users, it depends on a set of valued activities very different than those the Encyclopedia Britannica's creators engage in. In education, we are familiar with institutional methods: planning, scaling, overseeing, marketing, directing, incentivizing, and even mandating. (Sounds like traditional professional development, right?) Grassroots projects depend on a different process: looking for genuine needs, experimenting, pioneering, soliciting input, listening, testing, learning, adapting, reconfiguring, and even practicing benign neglect.

8. **You should never mandate participation, just encourage.** A network or online or physical event must fulfill some compelling needs. You can't expect people to come to your network just because you have a great idea for talking about something that you think is powerful enough to draw participants on its own. People need a reason to come that compels them, solves a problem that they care about, or offers the means to do something they have always wanted to do but could not. Finding friends for Facebook does that. Finding answers about how to use technology in the classroom does that. One more online book club may not.

9. **Learning spaces should be built for independence.** If your expectations or your network cannot survive someone choosing to leave your network and play somewhere else, you need to shift your mental model. Increasingly, the ability of learners to choose (which I like to refer to as *learner agency*) means that you need to support their choices by freeing them to move on without burdening them with the inference that they are breaking up your network. By making it clear to your members that you respect that agency, you will develop a positive culture within your network.

10. **Learning spaces should be a park, not a cafeteria.** When you build a park, you create spaces for people and activities, allowing for the community to use the spaces in ways that you might anticipate but can't fully control. The story is told that smart park designers wait to see where the natural paths get worn before constructing the permanent pathways and thus create structures that serve the users. In contrast, a cafeteria, while offering choice, typically has limited hours and set menus and requires the user to conform to the structure.

11. **It's important to start slowly.** Parks are often constructed in stages, starting with the equipment or facilities that the community can afford at the start and expanded as needs become apparent and more resources become available. This is a good model for communities. Don't worry if you're not experiencing wild growth. If you care about what you're doing, even just a few members having good conversation can sustain your interest for a long time, and that may be all that you need. If you grow larger and your community becomes helpful to more people, more power to you, but don't let anyone talk you into believing that you need to birth a full-grown community.

12. **Engagement trumps content.** That is, the topic or content is usually not as important as the act of engagement. One way to think about your park is to facilitate process, not outcome. Although you're not sure how

others will use the park, you try to put it in a convenient place and install features that will make it somewhere people will want to be. You do not care who exactly plays basketball with whom and when; you just want to make sure that parkgoers have the option to play.

13. **Allow engagement to determine direction.** New users will not be likely to understand the potential for social communities among peers. Once they have participated in a topic that they are interested in, and discover the power and opportunity, they will find other ways to engage. We each have dozens of things that we are passionate or care about. When we find a topic that engages us, that very engagement changes how we view our lives and sense of learning in all areas we are interested in. It changes how we think about sharing and discussing things with others. The corollary is that when a network we thought was going to be a big hit isn't, all is not lost.

14. **Events help build community.** To stretch the park analogy just a bit further, it helps to have community activities that encourage socializing, relationship building, and fun. In a park, you might have a barbecue or a tennis tournament; for an online social community, you might have an interview, a virtual field trip, a panel discussion, or the like. Tools like Google Hangouts make this kind of activity freely available.

15. **Learning spaces should be highly inclusive.** It's so very important to help those who are shy or unsure of themselves to participate. If the goal is helping to facilitate self-directing learners who contribute to each other's learning experiences, it is important to create a welcoming environment that respects the different levels of thought and preparation members bring. The sometimes competitive nature of formal education and the criticism of student work that is an inherent aspect of it result in large numbers of learners believing that they are bad at learning. For the benefit of these folks, and for the larger community as well, we have to help overcome this perception.

16. **Focus is critical.** This principle may seem to conflict with some of the flexibility and member agency we've been talking about, but it's an important balancing point. A community that doesn't have a defined, specific focus gives users little reason to return and participate.

17. **You need to be careful not to let the tail wag the dog.** Many of the structures and policies in top-down organizations and communities exist to standardize outcome, reduce workload, and serve clerical aspirations or hierarchical reporting more than they serve the needs of the individuals in

them. This mindset is fairly ingrained in us and is a temptation we have to overcome. Policies and procedures often take more time to create and manage than the work they are intended to avoid. This bias toward systemization has been particularly interesting to think about with regard to virtual conferences. Physical conferences are typically made up of so many policy-type requirements that they can block authentic opportunities to grow and change, and this is usually replicated in virtual conferences.

18. **Failures, especially your own, are a part of the building process.** The final piece of advice for structure and experience is that trying out new ideas means that, more than likely, some of them will not work out. If you feel badly about that, you will not take any chances. Allow yourself the opportunity to fail, then hold your head high and acknowledge the failure publicly. You will discover that mixed in with some of those experiments that don't go the way you wanted will be some gems that will exceed your expectations.

19. **It helps to practice benign neglect—the art of compassionate ignoring.** As the creator of a social learning community, you will be tempted to take charge when there is a difficulty or when things are going in a different direction than what you expected or intended. When you recognize that your role is primarily facilitating the growth and agency of others, you allow others to work through or solve difficulties or problems. As facilitator, you can and should encourage members of a healthy community to work together through questions, challenges, or struggles.

20. **Benign neglect requires patience.** Initiatives can take a while to work or catch on. If they don't, benign neglect is a way of letting go of responsibility and being willing to be comfortable with gaps or lulls in activity. It also avoids the overreactions that come from feeling responsible for everything all the time. It allows you to absolve yourself from responsibility of investing time into solving a problem that someone else created.

21. **Benign neglect creates space.** In traditional organizations, if you have an idea for a project or community, the accumulated weight of expectations (and sometimes dollars) invested in the idea can lead to a mindset of success at any price, even if you discover weeks or months later that it would actually be better to go in a different direction. Benign neglect includes a willingness to allow a community to languish if the interest or energy isn't there. Sometimes the emotional detachment that comes from benign neglect provides the opportunity to later re-engage the community when other factors or forces align to give the community increased relevance.

22. **Others need to be allowed to experiment and sometimes fail.** To the degree that you can, it's important to cultivate a personal tolerance for and a community facilitation of experimentation. You're not going to personally think of every good idea that would benefit your community; giving others the chance to try out new projects or ideas is the best way to keep your community vibrant. If a new project or idea doesn't achieve success, remember, you don't have to rescue it. You can practice benign neglect. Sometimes you lead, sometimes you follow, and sometimes you just get out of the way.

23. **Go, give, and get.** Institutional leadership carries a different set of priorities than grassroots facilitation, and *go, give, and get* is my personal formula for new projects. *Go* indicates the important weight of action in a world where there is an abundance of free community-building tools. Have an idea? Just start it. *Give* prompts us to do something that is authentically valuable to others. What topic, group, or opportunity would you uniquely benefit with your skill set or passions? What gift can you give to the community of people who share that same interest? *Get* is in last position. You do need to derive some takeaway for yourself in order to continue participating or leading. However, avoid predefining that benefit. Our quantifications (often financial) can limit our view of what our investment of time and energy can bring. For example, maybe the *get* is some form of career advancement. You might build key relationships with others who share motivations or a mission. Don't overlook the pure satisfaction of making a difference for others. However, letting this come to you after leading with authentic interest allows you to discover opportunities that you might not have seen if you predetermined what you thought you should get.

24. **Trust others.** Often the rules, procedures, and tracking in hierarchical institutions communicate a lack of trust in their members. We tend to believe everyone must follow some set of instructions. Unfortunately, this insistence on rigid adherence shows that we are more concerned about the outcome than the process, and that priority comes through loud and clear. Give opportunities for participation and growth, but structure things so that when some people do not take advantage of your supports, nothing actually falls apart. Create an environment where those who want to make a difference can do so and those who are not ready will see other chances down the line. This is much easier when you push responsibility downward.

25. **Responsibility should be pushed downward.** Institutional structures can often foster a culture of co-dependency. One of the great features of Ning networks is that they allow any person to start a conversation, or if the network creator has granted permission, to start a group. This provides terrific opportunities for self-starters to take action and gain appropriate recognition. In the virtual conferences I run, we ask prospective presenters to submit their presentations to the general conference network in a public forum, so that other members can comment on them, and we do not make spelling corrections for them or take responsibility for their quality. Those presenters we accept to present then schedule their own presentation time on a time-slot availability calendar. They are expected to attend one of the training sessions on how to use the software platform for presenting. We don't keep track of whether or not they attended—the proof is in the pudding, and an unprepared presenter may get negative feedback from participants who took the time to attend the session.

26. **When you push responsibility down, you accept that some people will not fulfill their responsibilities.** However, you don't have to take on those responsibilities for them. As one person, I managed almost all of the technical aspects of the Web 2.0 Labs' virtual events in 2012. I could never have done this without delegating responsibilities to the presenters. My advice: Let people rise and fall on their own, even while you are being supportive and understanding. Resist the temptation to take over, lest others miss opportunities for responsibility and growth. The cause of a lot of failure may stem from our fear that people will fail and how that reflects on us.

27. **The cruise director, not the ship's engineer, is the learning community's leader.** Cruise director Julie from *The Love Boat* is your role model, not Scotty from *Star Trek*. It's important to not confuse technical capability (Scotty) with social community leadership (Julie). Julie's job benefits most from emotional labor. Your ability to sense the fears and insecurities of new contributors, or the frustrations and confusions of more seasoned ones, is a skill that means much more in social learning community leadership than, arguably, anything else. A good community manager has empathy and can encourage social learning with even a mediocre technical platform, but the opposite is rarely true. If you are associated with an organization, and leadership asks for metrics to measure your community or your performance, make sure the measures put in place are not just simplistic (such as many new members have joined during a period of

time), but also involve qualitative feedback measures (such as testimonials of the impact of participation).

28. **Emotionally sensitive leadership often leads to visible or public kindness.** This significantly impacts the feel or tenor of a community for good. How you react to those in your community strongly determines how they will react to each other. Communities develop a recognizable character or quality that has an impact on the comfort of all participants, nurturing an environment of trust.

Conclusion

I hope that this exploration of what I've learned about creating and facilitating social learning spaces goes beyond being just another playbook for community building. Potentially, it illuminates broader elements of social learning. I hope the parallel nature of learning and learning environments for all involved in education—students, teachers, administrators, parents, and communities—strikes you.

The most important lesson of all may be the degree to which facilitating the learning of others depends most on understanding and modeling that mode of learning in ourselves. Take note of a typical flight attendant's safety announcement:

> In the event of a loss of cabin pressure, oxygen masks will automatically appear from the overhead bins. Place a mask over your nose and mouth and breathe normally. If you have young children with you, place the mask on yourself before assisting them.

You can't encourage another's learning unless you are learning yourself. As opportunities for learning have shifted dramatically out of the institutional buildings and onto the web, it will be very hard for us to help others navigate new learning opportunities without experiencing them ourselves.

There's a second reason for the airline directive about putting the oxygen mask on first. Children will be more willing to put something on their faces if they see that a trusted adult has done so first. This is modeling, and it's at the core of social learning. Intriguingly, the very tools that now allow us to learn across all kinds of previous boundaries are at the same time tools that allow our learning to be more visible, enabling us to teach from the inside out—modeling those learning traits we seek to inspire in others.

"You, first" is the best advice I can give you about leading social learning spaces. Since I've also said that it's not about you, it's about the learners in a community, it may seem like a Zen paradox to conclude with what seems like opposite advice. "You, first" means *you* experiment, *you* put yourself out there, and *you* become your own biggest experiment as a learner. Then, when you're ready to lead others, "You, first" transforms into *you* leading the way, respecting and supporting others, trusting and giving others responsibility, and helping them to build their own learning.

We have an opportunity, perhaps unique in the history of humankind, to engage in learning spaces at a democratic level. Technology has opened the door to this opportunity, but our ability to take advantage of the moment depends on reshaping our definitions of where, how, and by whom these learning communities are built. The *where* is inevitably *everywhere*. The *how* is what we hope we have begun to uncover. To define *by whom*, we must encourage all to participate.

References

Hargadon, S. (2008, March 4). Web 2.0 is the future of education [Web log post]. Accessed at www.stevehargadon.com/2008/03/web-20-is-future-of-education.html on June 5, 2013.

 **Marie Alcock** is president of Learning Systems Associates and serves as an education consultant in the United States and internationally. Her work focuses on the areas of curriculum, instruction, and assessment. She has spent over twenty years working in public and private education as a teacher, administrator, and public advocate. She is the founder of Tomorrow's Education Network, a nonprofit dedicated to connecting the greater community with students in the classroom to improve student literacy. Marie has been working with schools to improve student motivation and literacy skills through digital tools and gaming.

Marie is a coauthor of *Mapping to the Core: LivePlanner* and "A Virtual Continuum for Thinking Interdependently" in *The Power of the Social Brain: Teaching, Learning and Interdependent Thinking*. Marie has written a number of papers and articles about curriculum mapping, gaming, leadership, and organizational change.

She holds a doctorate in education research and a master's degree in the art of teaching. To learn more about Marie's work, follow her on Twitter @mariealcock, or visit www.lsalearning.com for more information.

To book Marie Alcock for professional development, contact pd@solution-tree.com.

Chapter 4
Gaming as a Literacy: An Invitation

By Marie Alcock

> *Existing models of literacy simply do not*
> *fully address reality in the world today.*
>
> —Eric Zimmerman

The truth is, video games are hard work, and learning to play one can be a frustrating experience. Many complex games can require over fifty hours of play time to reach "a win state." In addition, complex games often have a number of different win states, allowing a number of different solutions or strategies to be effective in solving the given problems. When a player has won using one strategy he or she will often replay the game using a new strategy. A game might have a win state reached by having the most points, the greatest amount of territory on a map, the most levels complete, or by having developed the strongest character (avatar). A player can be working toward several different win states at the same exact time. What is it about these games that encourages children and adults to work so hard at mastering them? Does something in this process point to the pleasure of working that all humans share?

Games support us through the learning process by giving us tasks that are matched to our skill level and are just hard enough to push us. Along the way, well-designed games tend to give us the content information we need just when we need it, so that the content has meaning for us and is immediately applied. Important knowledge is shared between the player and parts of the game play that give information we do not know already (in-game smart tools), which allow us to be active players before we are fully competent. (A simple example is that a video game about horse racing does not require the player to actually know how to ride a horse). In addition, there are different areas within games, with different ways of teaching how to play. In tutorials, training grounds, sandboxes, and scrimmages, we play the game in simplified versions and begin to know what it feels like, so we have a context for wanting to work hard to learn more. In these areas of the game we learn, hone, practice, and test skills before we attempt the real game. This process of learning exactly what we need to know when we need to know it is effective. There is something to having options about how we will learn that makes well-designed games effective at teaching a player how to play a hard game.

Finally, we as players are constantly given detailed feedback about where we are in the game and what we need to do to level up or beat the game. Having small skill steps aligned with clear feedback loops makes each level of an otherwise overwhelmingly large and complex game doable. For the educator, this is the equivalent of knowing where we are, where we are going, and exactly what we have to do to get there. Goal badges, experience bars, and leveled-up notification provide feedback to the players to keep their motivation up and to continue learning skills needed to beat difficult levels. As players, we have the sense of challenge and the thrill of seeing ourselves succeed where only days before we had no hope of winning. We are acutely aware of how far we have come. How do video games do this so well? How do they make learning so much fun? The key is in the design principles.

Video game makers have two basic design principles: (1) games that are too easy do not sell, and (2) games that can't teach the player quickly and effectively do not sell (Walker, 2003). As a result, the commercial market has designed products and processes to teach complex skills, rich content, and dynamic and multifaceted systems to players quickly and efficiently. These video games have design principles that make us want to learn hard things.

Along with books, television, movies, and art, video games are in almost every home, and almost every generation plays them. Video games are so enjoyable that people of all ages will work hard and dedicate hours of time to mastering them. Wouldn't it be wonderful if we could get that kind of response in the classroom—creating an addictive curriculum, if you will?

How would this look in the classroom? Just bringing in a video game does not work well. It is not the game alone that produces the educational equivalent of a slam dunk. The impact on student learning requires the teacher to plan for, select, align, and connect the game to the learning objectives of the unit. Because educators do not make off-the-shelf-games, we have to make the links to the learning explicitly clear to students.

Many educators are designing for-classroom-games that do this within the preK–16 curricula. Some are modifying features of off-the-shelf-games to fit the curriculum or creating affinity spaces (spaces where informal learning takes place) to maximize the learning of off-the-shelf-games. Others are having students design games, which develops student fluency in this complex literacy. Students are gaming inside and outside the classroom, in after-school clubs, on family gaming nights, and at schoolwide tournaments (see figure 4.1). An Internet search yields many examples of gaming in school, including the following.

- The Story and Game Academy (http://storyandgameacademy.pbworks .com)

- 3D GameLab Online Teacher Camps (http://3dgamelab.com/online -teacher-camp)

- *WoW in School: A Hero's Journey* and *15 Minutes of Fame: WoW Goes to English Class* (http://wowinschool.pbworks.com and http://wow .joystiq.com)

- MinecraftEdu and Minecraft in School (http://minecraftedu.com and http://minecraftinschool.pbworks.com)

- SimCityEDU (www.simcityedu.org)

In classrooms	• Aligned to standards • Building basic skills • Problem solving and taking action
In school	• Clubs and extracurricular activities • Community applications • Family gaming nights
Outside school	• Home • Friends' homes • Library

Figure 4.1: Where students are gaming.

However, there are video games, and there are *good* video games. Many games, particularly ones marketed to schools, fail to capture the attention of the learner (Gee, 2012). Many times, it is because they recreated the "read, view this section, and then interact with these questions" format. Simply having video images or being on the computer is not what makes a video game good for learning. So, it is important to identify the characteristics of a good video game for learning. James Paul Gee, cognitive scientist and baby-boomer-generation gamer, has worked extensively to do exactly this. In the 2012 Games for Change Festival keynote, he identified these rich gaming experiences as "big G games"—games that are designed as rich, motivational learning experiences (Gee, 2012). Big G games have all of the elements of gaming literacy and are a different experience from simply playing a video game. Some games allow players to build civilizations, run simulated businesses, role-play multifaceted characters, speak world languages in immersion simulations, and lead entire organizations of real people. It is the impact of these kinds of experiences on players that results in the first layer of deep learning.

The second layer of deep learning is found in the affinity spaces where players connect, communicate, compare, and create around the content of the game they are playing. No matter the genre or design type, these games connect their players, allowing beginners and experts to share, evaluate, and create together (Gee, 2003). This is done with no attention to the age, race, creed, or gender of the participants, only their commitment to learning more about the content. Good video games are effective at engagement, motivation, language development, and deep learning through the combination of strong design elements and strong affinity spaces. This is your invitation to enter the newest horizon in the field of education—gaming literacy—and to understand how it can take learning to the next level.

How Video Games Promote Learning

Although games can be immensely entertaining, it would be a mistake to consider them only a form of entertainment. Their real value is in how they balance problem solving and fun. They do this with a sense of hope that rests on a player's genuine belief that if he or she keeps trying, he or she will win. Jane McGonigal (2010), a game designer, captures this well in her TED talk titled "Gaming Can Make a Better World." She describes gamers as believers in the *epic win*—the notion that they can and will solve globally epic problems if they just work hard enough. Even in the face of repeated failure or rejection, gamers come back for one more try, because they are always so close to the next level. Anyone who has played *Super Mario Bros.* and repeatedly defeated Bowser only to find that the princess has been moved knows this dedication deeply.

Let's consider how this learning process is hardwired into the human brain.

Participatory Culture and Engagement

Video games are participatory, especially when compared with broadcast media or cinema, and a profound shift is occurring in what participation looks like. Digital development and production tools are changing how we interact with the creative and production processes. YouTube, GarageBand, and iMovie allow students to participate in the publication process without gatekeepers, and video games are often a guide to and scaffold for this kind of production. Gamers participate in online learning to get better at their video games, and they generate movies of their play for feedback as well as to provide guides or walkthroughs to *noobs*, or beginners. Players connect with experts and participate in fan fiction (writing stories about games) and mod creation (creating new versions of games) and often build new worlds, levels, or games of their own.

The dynamic combination of the game experience and the affinity space takes the learning experience to a deeper level. This is required for a big G game to be successful. Often, players post challenges and use game-design elements to simulate problems in order to find potential limits of the design properties. Middle or high school students might create challenge scenarios for one another in games that simulate resource management or in historical simulations such as *The Sims* or *Civilization IV*. Elementary students might share journal writing and step-by-step how-to guides for crafting techniques from *Minecraft* adventures. In fact, the amount of "how to beat this level" or "walkthrough" sharing is enormous in the affinity space and is an excellent place to start students in writing informational pieces. In fact, an educator can meet the Common Core State Standards for English language arts (NGA & CCSSO, 2010) using any genre game. The assignments in figure 4.2 can be completed with gameplay either in or outside the classroom.

Script	**Argument**
Create a script of a play, sequence of moves, tips, and descriptive directions to guide new player through a board. To be presented aloud while filming student actually demonstrates techniques.	Formulate an argument using details from text (game, dialogue, handbook, and so on) to support a change or modification to the game to make it better, easier, more challenging, or more historically accurate.
Game and Affinity Space	
Narrative	**Information or Research Piece**
Tell the story of a character from the game and describe the sequence either literally or creatively through the game environment. Extend the experience while staying within the parameters of the game-design elements.	Write an informational or research piece exploring the content of the game and either substantiating or denying the realism of the game's design, historical accuracy, or the physics involved with specific movements.

Figure 4.2: Possible video game assignments for Common Core State Standards for Writing.

The process of editing and revising written work is done through the postings in these affinity spaces, as well as through the use of high-frequency and domain-specific vocabulary. Physics, chemistry, mathematics, history, art, music, world language, and earth science are all topics in both commercial and independently designed games. The content of games has no limit; all of the different standards can be met. The challenge is for educators to learn more about good games and to make the connections for students in the classroom. The potential is there for us to tap. (One free resource for teachers is www.lsagames.com.)

Digital media make it easier and easier for students to find personally meaningful learning through participation in video games. Video games can be the realization of the theories of sound educational learning described by John Dewey and Maria Montessori (Squire, 2011). In fact, game designer Will Wright (*The Sims* and *Spore*) compares his games to Montessori toys (Wright, 2007). His games guide learners through cycles of discovery in the same way Montessori toys do. Wright's games and Montessori toys involve perceiving patterns and relationships through cycles of action, observation, and feedback. Both also assess understanding in a self-correcting way, as learners plan, fail, and revise. Assessments may be in the form of extended written responses in affinity spaces, performance tasks in quests, or personal communications in journals or postings. For young children, the use of touch technologies and the game interactions that take place there satisfy the same learning process. Children as young as two years old are interacting with games to learn the alphabet, animal sounds, rhythm, and colors.

Simulations

In the field of education, we are aware that seeing, knowing, and acting are deeply interconnected. When we approach a goal, we shift our thinking or lens to include everything we know about that goal and what affects it. So, if we are trying to align the curriculum in a school, we might shift our thinking among the following lenses to make sure we do not miss a part of our goal: curriculum maps, student achievement samples, types of students, environmental impacts, K–12 sequences, horizontal relationships per grade level, and so on. Video games train players and give them lenses to see the world this way, with various attributes and affordances. Players use their knowledge of these lenses to help them take actions toward their goals. This is the interconnected process of seeing, knowing, and acting taking place routinely within the design of a video game.

The power of a simulation is that it creates a world in which a player can take action risk free. Imagine a simulation through the Xbox wireless interactivity tools, where you can actually walk down a street in Paris and use your emerging French language skills to interact with the people there. The game design allows the AI (artificial intelligence) or NPCs (nonplayer characters) to "see" you and try to interact with you. As a player, one's goals are to engage with this immersion experience. This kind of simulation is available at the cellular level in biology and all the way up to global and cosmic simulations, as seen in the game *Spore*, where the player can act out evolutionary cycles, colonization cycles, ecological systems, sustainability systems, and economic systems.

A simulation allows players to interact with a complex system and test hypotheses about actions and reactions without the risks inherent in real-world systems. They give feedback to players about how they are learning and the effectiveness of their strategies. Gee (2008) makes the case that humans think and understand best when they can actually see (simulate) and experience content in such a way that the simulation prepares them for future needs. In this way, Gee suggests, effective thinking is just like running a simulation.

When thinking inside a game's rules and affordances, players are able to create lenses that allow them to minimize the risks and maximize the opportunities afforded by the rules and range of the game design. This is far more engaging than reading about the system or even viewing it in action through a static film. This ability to minimize and maximize the game design, test the boundaries, and see what can be done in a safe environment allows players to experience the world and train their own intuitions. Ultimately, the player is able to view the real world with this lens when he or she wants to.

Kurt Squire (2011), educator and gamer at the University of Wisconsin, and his team created a 3-D simulation game to help introductory physics students develop intuitive understandings of electrostatics. *Supercharged!* requires students to use electromagnetic fields to steer their spaceships through various levels of obstacles. After playing the game, students are able to visualize the relationships between electromagnetic fields even while walking down the hallway of their schools. Squire's point here is that games can effectively simulate any profession—science, architecture, sociology, and so on; there is no limit. These simulation games can promote learning to the intuitive level. Students are able to simulate the kinds of patterns, problems, or puzzles that any professional field would naturally encounter. Case study examples of this kind of work can be found in the book *Video Games and Learning* (Squire, 2011). Figure 4.3 (page 86) suggests some video game simulations for classroom use.

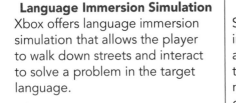

Language Immersion Simulation
Xbox offers language immersion simulation that allows the player to walk down streets and interact to solve a problem in the target language.

Urban Planning
SimCityEDU is a series of increasingly complex problems that address all of the STEM (science, technology, engineering, and mathematics) subjects through a complex virtual environment.

Simulations

Physical Phenomena
Using PhET Interactive Simulations, students can investigate physical phenomena in areas of biology, chemistry, earth science, mathematics, and physics.

Profession Simulation
The River City Project from Harvard University offers profession simulation. Students can be the scientist and mathematician as they fight disease transmission.

Figure 4.3: Possible video game simulations available for the classroom.

Collaboration and Cooperation

Games are based on problems to solve, not on content. This doesn't mean that game-based problem solving should eclipse learning content, but it does mean that a critical part of being literate in the digital age means being able to solve problems through simulations and collaboration. The collaboration has two levels: (1) collaborative play and (2) cooperative play.

Collaborative Play

Collaborative play is working together to solve a single-player challenge. As my son was working so hard to master *The Legend of Zelda: Twilight Princess*, which is a single-player game by design, he made use of his father, his uncle, YouTube, and a game bulletin-board site with hints and walkthroughs to help him learn at each step. This is sophisticated collaboration between beginners and experts. It also highlights the social nature of video gaming in the 21st century, even with a single-player game. No one tries to master these games alone; it is understood that when learning, we enlist the best of the best to support and model for us.

Students do not try to learn all by themselves; they work at a problem together until they figure it out. Then they proceed to work at trying to be the best at it in terms of performance. They return to the challenge again and again to master it in different ways. You can see this in video games like *Angry Birds*, as players replay completed levels to get all three stars, or when they try to win the bonus points in *Guitar Hero* or *Dance Dance Revolution*. It is also clear when we note the number of showcase videos on YouTube illustrating different ways to defeat Zant or Ganon in *The Legend of Zelda* series. This commitment to share strategies and guide new players unites the learning and assessment process. Students help one another become proficient (it is not fun to beat a player who does not know how to play the game), and then they compete for mastery levels and more elegant solutions to the problems.

Henry Jenkins (2006) suggests that students are actually being deskilled if they are learning this way and then returning to a classroom that is locked into a model of autonomous learning. Jenkins also notes that autonomous learning contrasts sharply with the kinds of learning that students need when entering the new knowledge cultures. Collaborative learning as seen in video games is a method of the future. An example is seen in the evolution of the game and how students are producing entire worlds, metagames (games within a game), and mods (new forms of the game), and publishing written and video pieces about the game on a professional and amateur level. What is it like for these students to return to a classroom where they are asked to study only what others have produced?

Cooperative Play

Cooperative gameplay combines puzzle pieces or differentiated access to information and codependent or interdependent goals. This combination allows the players to work together to defeat other teams or the game itself. In education, we know that having beginners and experts work together provides a *zone of proximal development* (Vygotsky, 1978). We witness this in all kinds of games, from online video games (*World of Warcraft* [*WoW*] and *Minecraft*) to table-top board games (*Pandemic* and *Forbidden Island Castle Panic*). Cooperative play builds deeper relationships between players as well as a safe environment for strategy testing and modeling. Video games, and the type of learning and thinking they generate, provide a space for cooperation between beginners and experts. The key is that the players are codependent on one another to reach a win state. The game most likely cannot be won alone.

Good video games may be able to overtly teach cooperation and collaboration, or *cross-functional teamwork* (Gee, 2008). Cross-functional teamwork combines both collaborative and cooperative play. In massively multiplayer online role-playing games like *World of Warcraft*, groups are composed of different character types, such as hunter, warrior, druid, or priest, who each play the game in a different way. Players interact with each other not in terms of their real-world characteristics but through their functional gaming identities. This video game design requires the players to band together at times to be successful against bosses or summative levels. They must learn about their own skill sets as well as those of the other types so as to maximize their impact as a group. For example, character types band together and win when they have warriors to fight a boss and druids to cure the warriors when they are injured. In *World of Warcraft*, banding together in a *raid* allows players to participate based solely on ability and not on any other real-world race, class, culture, or gender. See figure 4.4 for examples of *WoW* video game assignments.

Theater Events Hold theater events in the *WoW* environment. Act out scenes from *Romeo and Juliet* to a live audience in the game.	**Coordination and Leadership** Coordinate and lead raids with multiple languages and time zones. Use translation tools and world clocks to organize an event.
World of Warcraft	
Algorithms Use algorithms for statistics calculation and item use. New items change character statistics. Each rule of the game is a mathematical formula. Use mathematics to identify which characters should use which items.	**Character Development** Sample using character-development curriculum. Teams require players to know when to be a leader and when to follow directions. Players can experience both roles at different times.

Figure 4.4: Possible *WoW* video game assignments for grades 9–12.

Motivation

Games provide a journey that is emotional and profoundly deep. They are a doorway to deep learning when designed correctly. Players will commit to the game and work *very* hard to master the skills and content needed to win. However, education games, or *edutainment* games, have routinely sacrificed the quality of the win status by producing games that are nothing more than repurposed textbook content.

Players are not naturally gifted at gaming. They develop mastery through dedicated practice and participation in a cycle of expertise. This cycle is littered with dead ends, wrong turns, start overs, and game overs. Yet, players keep coming back for more, because games encourage a growth mindset.

The addictive nature of this extended cycle of expertise includes the feeling that one is *so close* to gaining the next level. (See figure 4.5.) The player is always, always improving and overtly aware of improvement. This might be seen through increased experience points, which can accrue and open more levels, options, or quests. It might materialize as badges, awards, and mastery levels, all of which open opportunities in the games or visibly improve performance (Sheldon, 2012). Everything a player does is either (1) actively building a new skill, (2) reaping the feel-good benefits of having built up a skill, or (3) facing a new and exciting challenge that clearly requires a new skill or combination of already learned skills. This process is never boring.

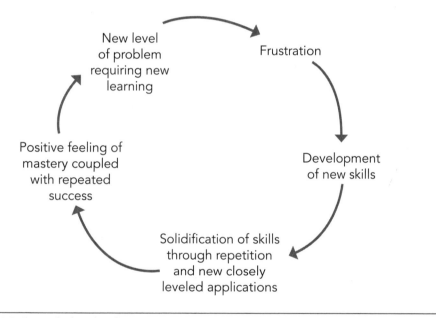

Figure 4.5: Extended cycle of expertise.
Source: Adapted from Gee, 2008. Used with permission.

If a video game is well designed, the leveling of the game allows for the player to experience a fine-tuned balance between the feelings of frustration and mastery. Remember, if a game is too easy or too impossible, it is no longer fun to play. No one likes to play a game when he or she feels as though it's impossible to learn enough to succeed. This is one definition of *at risk*, and it happens when one no longer has the motivation to try. The only one who can control this moment is the learner; he or she has a choice. Additionally, the variables impacting this moment are different for every learner every day. Good games leave room for this in the design, so at any moment a player can choose how to learn. These empowered learners are active in designing and getting feedback about their own learning process. They use what is known about how they learn to customize their experience. The empowered learners also seek to connect with their learning through identifying with a character of their creation (an avatar), either by attaching to an attractive identity available in the game or customizing their character's details. Finally, learners feel more expanded and powerful when they can manipulate tools in intricate ways that reach beyond their current limits, thus increasing their perceived effectiveness. This creates empowered learners (Gee, 2008). Table 4.1 models the empowered learner with sample games that align to each learning principle.

The Power of Choice

Quest games are a popular type of video game Facebook made exceptionally popular. These games do not typically have fancy graphics or complex interface designs. This format relies on the player feeling satisfied by the thrill of completing a quest, gaining experience or skill development, and then becoming more powerful. The design usually includes the following elements: (1) energy, (2) money, (3) health, and (4) experience. The player simply completes small quests to build experience points. Once players gain enough experience points, say by completing five quests, they level up and gain more energy, money, health, and experience. They are now more powerful in the game and can do more fun things. They also get more quests to complete, and the cycle continues. What appears as very simple is quite addictive, as it seems so easy to level up and get attractive power in the game. "You mean all I have to do is learn these skills, and I can really do all *that*?" "Yes, it really is that simple." Quests translate into the classroom as lessons or tasks (Haskell, 2012).

Using a game design similar to 3D GameLab (http://3dgamelab.com), one case study uses quest-based learning to motivate students to learn course material for a teaching course. Chris Haskell, a professor at Boise State University, explains the connection this way: "As quest-based learning activities involve student choice, the attractiveness of, and interest in, these self-selected learning activities play a role in the student's willingness to learn them" (Haskell, 2012, p. 2). He notes that students come to class at various levels of readiness to learn. They may be tired and prefer easier or shorter quests, while others may be ready for a challenge or want to dive into an engaging project. The ability to meet different readiness levels in the video game opens new doors in classrooms. Students can group in the classroom and turn to the teacher when they need support or walkthroughs or even work together to tackle a boss or summative quests. At the end of each quest, the players can give feedback on both personal and quest performance.

Table 4.1: Promoting Empowered Learners

Learning Principle	Importance	Game-Design Feature	Game Example	Education Connection
Codesign	Ownership, buy-in, and engaged participation	Players can take their own route through a well-designed game.	**Video Games** *The Elder Scrolls III: Morrowind, The Legend of Zelda series, Minecraft, Super Mario Galaxy, Sonic,* and *Pokémon* **Board Games** *Dixit, Dominion, 7 Wonders*	Learners make decisions about the curriculum. Students are part of designing their own learning.
Customized	Promoting learning styles and strengthening weaker learning styles	Game allows players to customize the gameplay to fit their learning and playing styles.	**Video Games** *Deus Ex* and *Deus Ex: Invisible War, Imperialism, Rise of Nations,* and *Civilization* **Board Games** *Puerto Rico* and *The Princes of Florence*	Students reflect on their own learning. Students have more than one way to solve problems.
Identity	Commitment	Good games offer either a character who is rich enough to motivate players or a character whose traits the player gets to create.	**Video Games** *Animal Crossing, World of Warcraft, Minecraft, FarmVille, The Adventures of Tintin, The Legend of Zelda* series, and *The Elder Scrolls III: Morrowind, Final Fantasy, Kingdom Hearts, Epic Mickey, Fable* **Board Games** *Dungeons and Dragons, Diplomacy*	Students get to really "be the scientist" or "be the mathematician" when working with the content and the skills.
Manipulation and Distributed Knowledge (Smart Tools)	Feeling empowered when manipulating powerful tools	Good video games offer characters or objects that the player can move intricately, effectively, and easily through the world.	**Video Games** *Heroes of Might and Magic III: The Restoration of Erathia, Tomb Raider, Rise of Nations, Prince of Persia, Bloons Defense, Plants vs. Zombies* **Board Games** *Pandemic, Ticket to Ride*	Learner is completely immersed in the world they are exploring and can take independent action within that world.

Source: Adapted from Gee, 2008.

Players want to make their own choices and give feedback to make the game better, balanced, fair, and fun. This is the foundation of quest-based learning (Haskell, 2012).

The 3D GameLab allows educators to build quests aligned to their curricula. These quests range from a minilesson format all the way to rich, project-producing quests. Haskell introduced me to some of the work that he has been doing with this kind of quest-based learning. One of his findings is that, if designed well, a curriculum could actually be addicting to the learner (Haskell, 2012). Figure 4.6 contains examples of quest-based learning.

In Haskell's study, the participants from a sixteen-week introductory educational technology course for preservice teachers met twice weekly for eighty-five minutes during the fall 2011 semester. The course used the 3D GameLab quest-based learning management tool that allows students the opportunity to participate in as many as sixty-six quests in six categories: context quests (eighteen), presentations (five), portfolio (nine), spreadsheets (four), web tools (twenty-three), and word processing (seven). Of the ninety-eight students who started the course, ninety-one completed with a grade worthy of advancement. If the submitted quest did not meet the requirements for acceptance, it was returned by the instructor with corrective instructions. This meant that all completed and approved quests earned the maximum point value, because students had the ability to resubmit quests that were not approved without penalty. As such, participants could continue working toward their desired grade, safely overcoming failed attempts in the process (Haskell, 2012).

Seven students did not complete the game for various reasons. All other students earned an A or A+. Students who received an A+ earned more than 10 percent beyond the required 2,000 experience points (XP) to reach a winning condition of the course; that is, they received greater than 2,200 XP or more. More than half of students who received an A continued to submit quests and received an A+. That means, 55 percent of the students continued to play the game, even after they had completed the course requirements (Haskell, 2012).

Gaming Literacy

When people learn to play video games, they are learning a new literacy. Video games are a perfect example of an evolving form of media that communicates distinctive and multifaceted types of meaning. The concepts at the heart of gaming literacy are: (1) systems, (2) play, and (3) design (Zimmerman, 2011).

1. **Systems:** There is a mathematical rule system that lies under the surface of every game. This is a formal structure, unlike that of most other media

Build Basic Skills	**Create Products**
Build basic reading and writing skills: Use Free Rice (http://freerice.com)—For each word students define correctly, twenty grams of rice go to the United Nations World Food Programme.	Create products: Use Read, Write, Rock! (www.readwriterock.com), where students get feedback from an award-winning creative director on their lyrics, song writing, genres, and styles.

Quest-Based Learning

Problem Solving	**Develop Machinima Piece**
Solve a given problem: Share and collaborate within an affinity space or guild from a simulation, using *Phoenix Quest*.	Use specific pieces of literature: Design, write scripts, and perform a machinima (drama or theatrical piece) with *LEGO City* or *WoW*.

Figure 4.6: Possible video game assignments in the 3D GameLab classroom.

types. To play, understand, and design games, one has to understand them as systems. Playing a game, testing strategies, modifying aspects, and then repeating is, in short, an iterative process that clearly exemplifies how games naturally and powerfully lend themselves to systems literacy.

2. **Play:** Systems become meaningful as people inhabit, explore, and manipulate them. Games are really social ecosystems. They are rich with the leveling of structures and human interaction, reflecting personal experience, invention, and transformation of the system. These dimensions are key aspects of a well-rounded literacy—a literacy based on play.

3. **Design:** Katie Salen and Eric Zimmerman (2003) define *design* as "the process by which a designer creates a context, to be encountered by a participant, from which meaning emerges" (p. 41). This brings us back to literacy as the understanding and creating of meaning and, in the case of game design, a set of possibilities. Because humans play the game using choice, the designer cannot possibly predict all possible patterns. Thus, unexpected things happen.

The ability to interact with the game design—in other words, "read" the design elements and then produce ("write") not only responses but also products—is a player skill set (Gee, 2003). This is one of the reasons students love playing video games. They are learning a new interactive language that grants them open access to virtual worlds that are filled with intrigue, engagement, and meaningful challenges.

> Literacy and even media literacy are necessary but not sufficient for one to be fully literate in our world today. There are emerging needs for new kinds of literacy that are simply not being addressed, needs that arise in part from a growing use of computer and communication networks. Gaming literacy is one approach to addressing these new sorts of literacies that will become increasingly crucial for work, play, education, and citizenship in the coming century. (Zimmerman, 2011, p. 24)

Gaming literacy is certainly not the only way to understand the changing world and its needs. However, using games and game design is one effective approach emerging both in and outside the formal classroom. Gaming literacy turns the tables on the way we think about games. Rather than focus on what happens inside the artificial world of a game, gaming literacy asks how playing, understanding, and designing games provide lenses for us to critically look at and effectively interact in the real world. Imagine all this potential learning in an intrinsically playful format. The playful format for a classroom requires the teacher and students to visualize problems as opportunities to simulate possible solutions, to connect and network with different experts, and to design new forms of interaction to witness a solution. There is play in the solution and in the classroom. Note that the requirement of a playful format applies to all kinds of games plugged or unplugged. Figure 4.7 features sample playful assignments.

Game and Education as a Design Science

We have seen video games motivate learners to work hard not just to master the gameplay to win but also to master the environment and design of the games in order to become designers in their own right. Players create new levels, fan fiction, new worlds, and characters with rich identity and back stories, reflecting the commitment the players have to the games they play. So, we must ask ourselves, "What is a strong, motivating game design?"

Where the educational designer is dedicated to end results, the game designer is focused on the user experience. To design effective classroom games, the designer must consider both. To do this effectively, the game design should align to the type of curriculum the player is expected to learn. To help do this, Dan O'Brien (2010) identifies four genres of educational games: (1) linear, (2) competitive, (3) role playing, and (4) strategic planning. It is important to remember that game

Build Basic Skills
Design (teacher or student) board games, card games, or scripts for video games about content being studied in class.

Role-Play
Use role-play to increase identity and commitment. Allow students to actually be the avatar from a game in class.

Playful Format

Level Up
Turn the classroom feedback loop into the game-design model. Have XP build up with each student's participation and allow students to level up and gain access to new materials.

Take Action
Have an impact in the local community by playing out a video game that predicts or simulates a problem, then share the results with the community in the form of a report.

Figure 4.7: Possible playful assignments based on game design principles.

classifications are not mutually exclusive, and many games represent elements of each in different ways. Figure 4.8 (page 96) shows how their taxonomy aligns to the learning tasks.

- Linear games are useful when teaching basic skills, which students will need later in more complex forms to solve problems. Tower defense games, such as *Bloons Tower Defense* or *Garden Defense*, are good examples of linear games, as they require the player to defeat the board using logic and problem solving. There is an opportunity to have students write solution walkthroughs and make mathematical arguments to support one defense on a board over another. In one classroom, we had second graders make mathematical arguments based on the tower defense game *Garden Defense*. Students used the costs to upgrade gnomes in the garden, compared to the costs to purchase many basic gnomes when defending a specific garden. Second graders were eager to do the mathematics and then argue abstractly and quantitatively to describe why their strategy would work.

- Competitive games are useful when teaching students to think on their feet in order to apply their skills in a real-time simulation. They must pay attention to their own ideas as well as the ideas and plans of others. Card games like *Dominion* require the players to build vocabulary, reading, and mathematics and are therefore wonderful transdisciplinary experiences. Games such as *Blokus*, *Candy Land* (with new curriculum-based cards),

Linear games require step-by-step logic for the player to beat the game. This would include drill-and-practice games for skill building and simulation-based games.

Competitive games require the same step-by-step logic but add a need for the player to anticipate the actions of other live or AI-controlled players to advance. This would also include cooperative group games and action or real-time games.

Role-playing games require the player to develop and maintain a complex character or identity within a real social or AI social environment to reach given and personal goals to advance or win. Students can build appreciation for real-world tasks.

Strategic-planning games require the player to either generate or maintain complex systems including the micromanagement of numerous levels of a system to advance through the game. Students are required to show information analysis, synthesis, and planning.

Figure 4.8: Four genres of educational games.

and *Railroad Tycoon* used in a social studies room are perfect examples of these kinds of games. Teachers should use competition carefully; what motivates some can intimidate others. *Pandemic* is an amazing competitive game that requires the players to work together as specific specialists (dispatcher, medic, scientist, researcher, or operations specialist) to defeat a disease before it spreads around the world. This competitive game pits a team of students against the problem of the game.

- Role-playing games focus on identity and a complex environment to work in to solve problems. These can be computer based as in *The Sims* games or online worlds like *World of Warcraft*, or students can make them up in table-top role-playing games. Having avatars for certain classroom lessons opens the door for students to imagine themselves as scientists, mathematicians, or urban planners. *Skylanders* is a role-playing game that attracts all learners. They can build the experience of a character and then watch as he or she does amazing things in the rich world of Spyro. In one classroom, students wrote a back story for their characters or finished the story of a character after a certain point in the game. This creative or narrative writing has a rich world to work in, and the students post their work in an affinity space that the teacher controls.

- Strategic-planning games are some of the most difficult and rewarding. The most common type involves resource management, as seen in the game *The Settlers of Catan*. Students can play and replay board games like *Puerto Rico*, *The Princes of Florence*, and *Diplomacy* to hone their techniques and strategies. Video games like *StarCraft*, *Civilization*, and *Spore* allow students to build vast empires and manage resources in very complex systems. Many schools have gaming clubs built around these kinds of games where affinity spaces have been created for students to compare techniques and strategies. Often these clubs host tournaments and family game nights where members can share their interests and teach community members how to play these very difficult games.

All four genres have representations in both plugged and unplugged versions. For example, the board game *Puerto Rico* is also a video game played against an AI or online human player. There is a card-game version called *San Juan,* as well. So, it is possible to build a classroom assignment like the following around the board game that has a component based on the video game version played at home:

Sample Assignment for Grades 6–10

Design a strategy tutorial around one resource or combination of resources in the game *Puerto Rico*. Name and describe the gameplay sequence that the player will use. In your description, you must use details from the game vocabulary and reference the roles indigo, sugar, coffee, tobacco, and corn played in the economies of the South American plantations correctly. The player should understand why each resource is valued differently in the gameplay. Make a mathematical argument defending the use of one resource over any other to reach a win state. Be sure to use details from the mathematics unit on ratios and percentages in your explanation. Test your strategy against the computer AI in the video game. Your strategy must win at least five out of ten games when a player follows your strategy. Name and describe a common counterstrategy and suggest adjustments to your strategy if faced with it in gameplay. Reflect on the following question as part of this assignment: Why is using a strategy different with a human opponent than with a computer AI? Your strategy must be presented on the wiki dedicated to resources management.

A Note on Bias

Games are biased by design. When designing a game, there are values applied to the possibilities and choices in the gameplay. The algorithms and affordances the design uses control the relationships between the game pieces and thus the possibilities for acting. In other words, because games are fundamentally mathematical formulas and computer programs following a flowchart of choices, the options are limited. The game designer's biases are as real to the player as an author's biases are to a reader.

We see this in Will Wright's *Spore*, which simulates the conditions that result in global warming destroying the planet, and again in *Civilization*, which Kurt Squire (2011) used to teach the process of historical and cultural development to middle school students. He used this game in his classroom in traditional lessons and in an after-school club. Not all of the students had the historical background knowledge that the game tapped into, but they began to ask questions about the history and use the domain-specific vocabulary when asked to describe the strategies they were using to be effective in the game. This opened the door for Squire and his colleagues to maximize the accurate content and address some of the limitations the game had to work within to be playable. *Civilization I, II, III,* and *IV* had to sacrifice certain details or adopt certain assumptions to host the games effectively; one assumption is that researching new technologies progresses society in a good way.

These biases are unavoidable when we create such games; they are committed to reflecting processes, not just facts. The logical extension of this position is that playing noneducational games can deliver the skills of probability theory and basic algebra when a win state requires figuring equipment tables and character statistics. In other words, the *content* of the game was Roman civilization, but the *skills* developed in the player through the process were algebraic. However, there is a way to resolve the impact of biased design features on students when games are used as learning tools: Be sure to have the students interact and learn from a variety of different games. Be sure that students are aware of the biases they are experiencing and that you encourage them to compare, contrast, and think about what they believe and ultimately how they will take action going forward.

Plugged and Unplugged

The truth is, the more we study the power of all kinds of games (for example, card, board, dice, video, table-top, or live-action role-play), the more we learn about the elements that make them effective, and the more easily we can recreate those elements in classrooms. Games do not need to be plugged in to promote learning. Lee Sheldon, an associate professor and codirector of the Games and Simulation Arts and Sciences program at Rensselaer Polytechnic Institute, explores this idea in his book *The Multiplayer Classroom: Designing Coursework as a Game* (Sheldon, 2012). Sheldon suggests that the multiplayer classroom is a game in its own right, and he has been developing courses using gaming techniques. Can a game be as effective without purchasing software, plugging anything in, or having even one computer? Will it work for every subject, grade level, or student? This has yet to be determined, but Sheldon (2012) suggests there is no reason *not* to think so. However, when designing a multiplayer classroom game, two lessons have already been learned.

1. Good games or big G games in the real world can be as compelling and as addicting as any video game mentioned in this chapter. I am reminded of the gaming conference DexCon at which people played live role-play and table-top games of all kinds. There was a little side game called *The Nexus* that attendees played as an amusement between "real games." Players were so committed to their characters that a separate convention was hosted dedicated to *The Nexus*.

2. Games played in the real world in real time demand flexibility. Gamers cannot depend on weather, human players, and NPCs to behave or play the way they do in a video game. The game master must write and design on the fly. This can be done on any game board, including your classroom, but classrooms should be ready to play a living, breathing game. It can help to play video games and role-playing games in preparation for such a powerful adventure.

As educators begin using game-design elements to transform their classrooms into live games, more research will be available to expand these recommendations. Figure 4.9 (page 100) gives some examples of unplugged video game assignments.

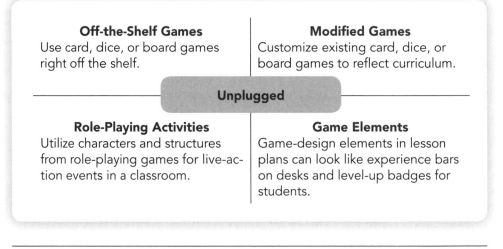

Off-the-Shelf Games
Use card, dice, or board games right off the shelf.

Modified Games
Customize existing card, dice, or board games to reflect curriculum.

Unplugged

Role-Playing Activities
Utilize characters and structures from role-playing games for live-action events in a classroom.

Game Elements
Game-design elements in lesson plans can look like experience bars on desks and level-up badges for students.

Figure 4.9: Possible unplugged video game assignments.

Students Designing Games

In the field of education, we have come to understand that learners should have clearly visible opportunities to become leaders, teachers, or authors in the disciplines they are studying. Kurt Squire (2011) writes:

> It should be clearly communicated what players must do to become experts, and they should have opportunities to interact with such experts regularly. By contrast, school functions to isolate students by age ability, filters all information through the teacher, and features few opportunities to interact with experts, much less become one. (p. 45)

Game design is hard work and by definition interdisciplinary. Making a game includes mathematics for a rules system; psychology for designing a human play experience; social studies for the cultural and social context for both the player audience and any storylines, logistics, aesthetics, sequencing, storytelling, writing, communication, visual and audio performance design, cultural art connections, entertainment design, or popular media; and computer and technological literacy for programming. This process, this design commitment, represents multimodal forms of learning and investigation. The process is one of the many layers of feedback and iteration. Two good resources to use when you begin are Jesse Schell's (2008) *The Art of Game Design* (2008) and Atsusi "2c" Hirumi (2010) *Playing Games in School: Video Games and Simulations for Primary and Secondary Education.* Consider the websites in table 4.2 to find games aligned to your content areas or grade levels. Use these resources to follow game releases and find out how other educators are using them in their own classrooms, but since new studies and resources come out every day, the best way to find resources is to search online using the search term "games in schools" or "games in education."

Table 4.2: Resources for Video Game Design

Serious Game Classification (http://serious.gameclassification.com)	Learning Village (www.learningvillage.com)
Through the Glass Wall (http://mathequity.terc.edu/gw/html/gwhome.html)	World Village (www.worldvillage.com)
Games in Education (http://gamesined.wikispaces.com)	SuperKids (www.superkids.com)
Games in Education Resources (http://gamesinedresources.wikispaces.com)	Joystiq (www.joystiq.com/games)

A game designer conceives and designs the rules and structure of a game. An educator can design learning experiences for students around these same types of rules and structures. There are six design roles—(1) lead designer, (2) systems designer, (3) environment designer, (4) writer, (5) user-interface designer, and (6) aesthetic designer—that are consistent regardless of the age of the student:

1. The **lead designer** coordinates the work of other designers as a project manager and is the main visionary of the game. The lead designer ensures team communication, makes large design decisions, and presents the design outside of the team. Keeping well-presented documentation also falls within the lead designer's responsibilities. This role creates the content design including: backstory, setting, and themes of the game. There can be additional designers if the range of the game is large enough.

2. The **systems designer** designs and balances the game's rules to keep them fair. This person must monitor the algorithms that define interactions in the gameplay as well as mathematical patterns within the game. This is the heart of the game's mechanics. Rules or game mechanics that are faulty can potentially break the system and result in players abandoning the whole enterprise. The system designer's role requires beta testing, or practice runs with test groups to eliminate bugs, to provide adequate feedback about each rule. Often, this will continue during gameplay, as players begin to mod or patch new pieces into the game; it is the systems designer that will *nerf*, or make weaker, any pieces that break or overpower the system.

3. The **environment designer** is responsible for creating an engaging game environment. The designer ensures that levels are appropriately matched

to the players' skills at each point in the game. This role should include documenting exactly where the player is in the cycle of expertise at all points in the game. The environment designer can make flowcharts of the optional routes and decision trees.

4. The **writer** is responsible for the story narrative, dialogue, commentary, cut scenes narrative, journals, packaging, hint systems, smart tools, and text props of the game. It is the responsibility of the writer to collaborate with primary designers to seamlessly place this content into the game, creating immersion, avoiding repetition, providing feedback, and so on. Writing for games involves a different set of skills than those needed for writing traditional works, such as novels or screenplays, as the writer must collaborate with the other designers during the writing process.

5. The **user-interface designer** is responsible for the usability and functionality of the game. The construction of the menus, views, display screens, feedback tools, and interaction tools would be a part of this role. Ease of play is very important for player satisfaction. This role would also require beta testing to gauge and refine the interface design.

6. The **aesthetic designe**r is responsible for the attractiveness and overall look of the game. The design of the board, screens, backgrounds, play pieces, characters, colors, music, sounds, design on nonplayer characters, and so on would all be a part of this role.

Consider the sites in table 4.3 to help you get started making your own video games for the classroom. These kinds of sites can have networks of teachers working to align curriculum with games or online tools. Begin with the free sites, and then consider a membership with a network of teachers willing to share and give feedback on this process.

Table 4.3: Resources to Make Games for the Classroom

Free Websites	Membership or Community Websites
ClassTools (www.classtools.net)	Quia (www.quia.com/web)
Hot Potatoes (http://hotpot.uvic.ca)	ContentGenerator (http://contentgenerator.net)
	Classroom management game (www.classdojo.com)

Games for the Classroom

Use the list in table 4.4 to start thinking about the possibilities that are out there. (Visit www.lsagames.com for more information.)

Table 4.4: Choosing Video Games for the Classroom

Subject Area	Game	Grades
Mathematics	3D Thinking Lab	2–8
	Little Bill Thinks Big	PreK–3
	Super Tangrams	5–8
	Zoo Tycoon	4–6
	3rd World Farmer	3–12
Social Studies	Real Lives	4–12
	Global Conflicts: Peacemaker	7–12
	SimCity 4	5–12
	Age of Empires	7–12
	Rise of Nations	7–12
	Europa Universalis	7–12
	Birth of America and Birth of America II	5–12
	Mindbender	9–12
	Carmen Sandiego	4–8
	Oregon Trail	5–8
Language Arts	Charlotte's Web: Word Rescue	PreK–3
	Furious Frogs	2–5
	GameGoo	PreK–K
	Lemony Snicket's A Series of Unfortunate Events	4–6
	Reader Rabbit	K–4
	The Legend of Zelda	4–6
	BioLogica	9–12
	Second Life	4–16

Continued →

Subject Area	Game	Grades
Science	SimCalc	6–8
	Harvest Moon: A Wonderful Life	PreK–3
	Race to Mars	6–12
	Minecraft	3–16
	Whyville	5–9
	Portal	7–16
	Gizmos and Gadgets	4–12
Physical Education	Dance Dance Revolution	All ages
	Wii Fit	All ages
	Kinect	All ages
	EyeToy	All ages
	GameBike	All ages
Music and Art	StaffWars	4–8
	JokaydiaGRID	4–6

Policies for Safety of Students Online

Although not all video games are violent, many educators are nervous about encouraging video games because there is a perceived connection to violent themes. *Wii Fit* has sold as many copies as every version of *Halo* ever made, or more. *The Sims*, which represents a simulation of everyday life, are among the most successful video games ever made. Finally, *Rock Band*, *Brain Age*, and *Alchemy* all avoid violent themes. Sports, racing, music, puzzle, adventure, role-play, and simulation games are the largest body of gameplay, representing 57 percent of teenage gameplay, according to the University of Stanford's Digital Youth Project in November of 2008.

To nurture the learning power of video games, educators must therefore open the access to powerful affinity spaces for students to participate in Big G games and work online with experts. Anne Collier, executive director of NetFamilyNews, collects research concerning safety and kids on the Internet. In her keynote address at the Games in Education conference in Troy, New York, in August 2012, Collier challenged us to address the negative and incorrect perception that screen time on the Internet is at best only entertainment and at worst dangerous.

> We need to help our children see that, in social media, they're stakeholders in their own and each other's well-being and that skilled, literate use increases well-being. It's a dilemma, certainly—we want to protect them—but the more we can show them our confidence in them, the more motivated they'll be to take ownership of their safety in and with digital media.

The public media message has been that *all* children are potential victims online. There is a fear in our culture that all children are in imminent danger as soon as they are exposed to the Internet. What is our role as educators in protecting students, while providing the access that will enable them to become digital citizens? It is to teach students how to navigate, search, and participate as stakeholders on the Internet. The future of Internet safety for students requires a combination of digital literacy skills and digital citizenship skills. The following are suggestions on how you can ensure students are safe, ethical, and efficient digital citizens.

- **Release control.** That may sound strange to those who fear for their students. However, control relies on providing extrinsic rewards for following the rules. Rules are important, but shared values build the capacity for intrinsic rewards. Having both extrinsic and intrinsic rewards is the key to a collaborative culture in a classroom. As educators, we usually use a range of external and internal rewards, but we know that the ultimate goal is self-control and self-regulation.

- **Support autonomy.** The power of choice extends here when meaningfully connected to specific goals, values, and a sense of identity. When students are able to identify what they are doing, why they are doing it, and how it brings meaning to their work or expression, they teach all of us about new forms of media and technology. This is why it is so important for all members of the community to understand what our students like about the media they use and why.

- **Create a safe space.** Physical safety is a baseline. However, when referring to digital spaces—spaces that have mutual trust and offer freedom to be silly, embarrass oneself, experiment with new concepts, fail, and try again—game scholars tend to stress psychological safety (Jones & Finkelhor, 2011). This kind of safety promotes all kinds of learning. (For more information about the online safety of children, follow the research from the Crimes Against Children Research Center [www.unh.edu/ccrc] and ConnectSafely [http://connectsafely.org].)

- **Model what you want to see.** Psychologists tell us that the will and participation of an entire school community is needed to defeat bullying; this is why risk-prevention experts focus so much on bystanders (Rossen & Cowan, 2012). Everybody and everything are keys to the climate and context of the community, from social games to families to schools. There is great advantage if we all learn how to play and engage in the media forms our students are using. The best thing we can model is how to be a professional learner, because this will serve our students throughout their lives.

Conclusion

Cooney Foundation (2012) reports that 32 percent of teachers use games two to four days a week. Cost, access to computers, and emphasis on standardized testing are barriers to using games in schools. If we heed the message that elements of video games show a pathway (one of many) to meaningful learning, and one that motivates and engages 21st century learners in deep ways, then new forms of formal schooling must be explored. We will also need to support educators and learners in how to cultivate the learning and evidence from this kind of complex learning process. This support begins with educators embracing the role of professional learner. By *professional learner*, I mean someone dedicated to learning not just in the exploratory ways we attribute to lifelong learners or through the modeling process of the public learner but in the professionalized, determined way we as researchers and agents of innovation learn about a problem and generate possible solutions. The professional learner is often gaming literate. How do you begin? Consider the following nine steps.

1. **Have your students collaborate with others to analyze and interpret games, as well as share strategies.** Through collaboration and networking, students can learn to enhance their own perspectives and ideas and contribute to our evolving knowledge culture. They will become systems literate.

2. **Play games.** Otherwise, how can educators have meaningful conversations about them? The Massachusetts Institute of Technology, Princeton, and the University of Wisconsin dedicate hours of playtime for their research teams, mathematics professors, and learning labs. They build play into their professional practice by design.

3. **Make connections between games and books, movies, TV, and the world.** By thinking about games beyond their boundaries, students can cultivate pattern recognition across media platforms and link the problem solving of gaming to the real world (plugged or unplugged).

4. **Design games with your students; make, play, and mod games.** Thinking about games as a designer will quickly launch you into the gaming world and equip you with the tools you need to advance in the game.

5. **Select a game to integrate into the curriculum.** Be sure to play the game and rate it on several levels. If the story is weak, the students will get bored. Does it really align to your curriculum standards? Is it appropriate for the age of your students? The Entertainment Software Rating Board (www.esrb.org/ratings/ratings_guide.jsp) has created a system to help, using *EC* for early childhood (ages three and up), *E* for everyone, *E+10* for children ages ten and older, *T* for teens thirteen and older, *M* for mature audiences, and *A* for Adults only (ages eighteen and up). Read reviews of the game online to find out how other teachers are using the game.

6. **Plan for and maximize the addiction aspect.** Answer these questions: (1) What part of your curriculum do you want the students to become addicted to? (2) What elements of the curriculum do you find students are not retaining or transferring the way you would like them to? Then, work to design a big G game that utilizes or focuses on those elements, and let the addiction to learning begin.

7. **Create the learning plan.** Students will not automatically see the connections just by playing; design activities to support the integration of the game experience into the learning experience. Ask the following questions:

    a. Do I understand the overall purpose of the game?

    b. Do I understand what my students should end up knowing, being skilled at, caring about, or being motivated to do after working through the game?

    c. Does the video game align with the intended learning objectives and standards I wish to address?

    d. Can the game provide experiences that existing classroom practices and activities cannot?

    e. Is there any research, or are there any reviews or outside evidence of this game being used to support student learning? If not (and that is frequently the case), am I prepared to explain the curricular relevance to students, parents, and leadership?

8. **Communicate with your leadership and technology support about the use of games in your classroom.** You need to present a clear plan for implementation, including a proposed technology contract for students

and parents before you introduce the game. There are valid concerns about playing video games in classrooms. When using repurposed games, you need to have played the game yourself to be certain you are aware of any violent or sexual or adult content embedded in the product. The technology support in your school will need to know what you are planning in order to ensure that the school's system meets the game's requirements. Will you need permission to install software on the computers? Is there an online component that a firewall might block?

9. **Communicate with parents and caregivers about the learning plan you have designed linking the video game to the standards.** Once you have a clear plan in place, you should begin formal meetings with parents to outline what you are doing and why you feel it will help students. When parents are given this kind of preface to the work, their fears and concerns can be approached professionally. To keep expectations and official policies clear for all members of the community, many schools use acceptable-use contracts and parent information letters about the kinds of technology that will be used. We encourage teachers to have alternative learning activities for students who choose not to play (or do not have parental consent to play) a video game.

Although video games have great potential to be powerful vehicles for learning, there is no guarantee this will happen, in the same way that there is no guarantee a student will understand the deep themes and powerful symbols of a significant work of literature when he or she first reads it. Thus, students need us and their peers to engage their gaming in thoughtful ways, to discuss and question around the problems, themes, designs, systems, and stories involved in playing and winning complex games. If good teaching always leads to learning, then please consider this your invitation to let the good games begin.

References and Resources

Collier, A. (2012, September 11). What Net safety can learn from digital game design [Web log post]. Accessed at www.netfamilynews.org/what-net-safety-can-learn-from-digital-game-design on August 30, 2012.

Entertainment Software Rating Board. (2013). *ESRB ratings guide.* Accessed at www.esrb.org/ratings/ratings_guide.jsp on November 1, 2013.

Fortugno, N., & Zimmerman, E. (n.d.). *Learning to play to learn: Lessons in educational game design.* Accessed at http://ericzimmerman.com/files/texts/learningtoplay.htm on June 7, 2012.

Gee, J. P. (2003). *What video games have to teach us about learning and literacy.* New York: Palgrave Macmillan.

Gee, J. P. (2008). *Good video games and good learning: Collected essays on video games, learning, and literacy.* New York: Peter Lang.

Gee, J. P. (2012, July 1). *Games for change: Keynote speech on affinity spaces* [Video file]. Accessed at www.bing.com/videos/search?q=games+for+change+keynote+2012&FORM=VIRE4#view=detail&mid=775D75575A99CB8CE0A5775D755 75A99CB8CE0A5 on November 1, 2013.

Haskell, C. (2012). *Design variables of attraction in quest-based learning.* Unpublished doctoral dissertation, Boise State University. Accessed at http://scholarworks .boisestate.edu/cgi/viewcontent.cgi?article=1286&context=td on November 1, 2013.

Hirumi, A. (Ed.). (2010). *Playing games in school: Video games and simulations for primary and secondary education.* Eugene, OR: International Society for Technology in Education.

Ito, M., Horst, H., Bittanti, M., Boyd, D., Herr-Stephenson, B., Lange, P. G., et al. (2008). *Living and learning with new media: Summary of findings from the Digital Youth Project.* Chicago: John D. and Catherine T. MacArthur Foundation. Accessed at http://digitalyouth.ischool.berkeley.edu on November 1, 2013.

Jenkins, H. (2006). *Convergence culture: Where old and new media collide.* New York: NYU Press.

Jones, L. M., & Finkelhor, D. (2011). *Increasing youth safety and responsible behavior online: Putting in place programs that work.* Washington, DC: *Family Online Safety Institute.*

McGonigal, J. (2010, March). *Jane McGonigal: Gaming can make a better world* [Video file]. Accessed at www.ted.com/talks/lang/eng/jane_mcgonigal_gaming _can_make_a_better_world.html on June 5, 2013.

McGonigal, J. (2011). *Reality is broken: Why games make us better and how they can change the world.* New York: Penguin Press.

National Governors Association Center for Best Practices & Council of Chief State School Officers. (2010). *Common Core State Standards for English language arts and literacy in history/social science, science, & technical subjects.* Washington, DC: Authors. Accessed at www.corestandards.org/assets/CCSSI_ELA%20Standards .pdf on August 15, 2013.

O'Brien, D. (2010). A taxonomy of educational games. In Y. Baek (Ed.), *Gaming for classroom-based learning: Digital role playing as a motivator of study* (pp. 1–23). Hershey, PA: Information Science Reference.

Rossen, E,. & Cowan, K. C. (2012). *A framework for school-wide bullying prevention and safety.* Bethesda, MD: National Association of School Psychologists.

Salen, K., & Zimmerman, E. (2003). *Rules of play: Game design fundamentals.* Cambridge, MA: MIT Press.

Schell, J. (2008). *The art of game design: A book of lenses.* Burlington, MA: Elsevier.

Sheldon, L. (2012). *The multiplayer classroom: Designing coursework as a game.* Boston: Course Technology.

Squire, K. (2011). *Video games and learning: Teaching and participatory culture in the digital age.* New York: Teachers College Press.

Vygotsky, L. S. (1978). *Mind in society: The development of higher psychological processes* (M. Cole, V. John-Steiner, S. Scribner, & E. Souberman, Eds.). Cambridge, MA: Harvard University Press.

Wright, W. (2007, July). *Spore, birth of a game* [Video file]. Accessed at www.ted.com /talks/will_wright_makes_toys_that_make_worlds.html on November 1, 2013.

Zimmerman, E. (2011). *Gaming literacy: Game design as a model for literacy in the twenty-first century.* Accessed at http://ericzimmerman.com/files/texts/Chap_1 _Zimmerman.pdf on June 7, 2012.

Bill Sheskey is the director of instructional technology for the Charlotte-Mecklenburg Schools in Charlotte, North Carolina, and a Curriculum 21 faculty team member. Bill designs and facilitates workshops nationally and internationally that provide hands-on experience in the development of authentic assessment strategies, essential question writing, and the use of web 2.0 tools, and guides educators in the design of high-quality curriculum upgrades that produce rich and relevant curriculum in all content areas.

Bill is a contributing author to Heidi Hayes Jacobs's *Curriculum 21: Essential Education for a Changing World*. His writing focuses on connecting with tech-savvy students and engaging them with the communication tools that they use in their daily lives.

Bill holds a master's degree in instructional technology and a specialist certificate in online learning and distance education. To learn more about Bill's work, follow him on Twitter @billsheskey.

Marie Alcock is president of Learning Systems Associates and serves as an education consultant in the United States and internationally. Her work focuses on curriculum, instruction, and assessment. She is the founder of Tomorrow's Education Network, a nonprofit dedicated to connecting the greater community with students in the classroom to improve student literacy. Marie has been working with schools to improve student motivation and literacy skills through digital tools and gaming.

Marie is a coauthor of *Mapping to the Core: LivePlanner* and "A Virtual Continuum for Thinking Interdependently" in *The Power of the Social Brain: Teaching, Learning and Interdependent Thinking*.

She holds a doctorate in education research and a master's degree in the art of teaching. To learn more about Marie's work, follow her on Twitter @mariealcock or visit www.lsalearning.com for more information.

To book Bill Sheskey or Marie Alcock for professional development, contact pd@solution-tree.com.

Chapter 5

The Classroom Website: A Marketplace for Learning

By Bill Sheskey and Marie Alcock

Olivia is entering seventh grade, and her parents are looking for a way to motivate her to improve her grades and take a greater interest in her own learning. They give her a smartphone, which has an Internet connection and all of the social media applications that Olivia wants to use to communicate and share information with her peer group. She is delighted.

Richard Bellows is Olivia's mathematics teacher. He realizes that almost every one of his seventh-grade students is using a phone or some device to communicate, so he is now learning about classroom websites. The previous summer, he participated in a professional development workshop, which guided him in the construction of a classroom website. Richard wanted to create 24-7 learning connections with his students using the devices that the majority had all of the time or, at the very least, had access to at home.

Richard creates a marketplace for learning and uses some basic elements to attract students to the site. He includes a calendar, newsletter, student network, challenge activities, parent connection, and school community center. Although he knows his options are limitless, he commits to building specific digital and media literacies. The site focuses on information organization, social networking, and digital citizenship.

Richard coaches his students to access the assignment calendar, video tutorials, student network area, current project support with hyperlinks to resources, and parent newsletter. Olivia and her classmates are impressed with the classroom website and appreciate the fact that Richard really cares about helping them achieve success in his class using the devices that are an integral part of their daily lives. Even though cell phone use is still restricted in school, Richard and his seventh-grade mathematics class are blurring the time between the school day and the rest of the day, where learning continues.

This example portrays the classroom website as a marketplace for learning, because it has the variety and flexibility of a thriving market. The availability of a variety of information and learning material 24-7 for all of the members of the learning community is immense. Students can get information about assignments, parents are able to get information about the classroom, administrators obtain information about the curriculum and instruction, and the public is able to access information about schools. The richness of the information makes the variety factor of the market powerful.

Then, there is the flexibility of the market. The website can connect different elements of the learning community in different ways. Students can work on projects or assignments together in wikis or social networking hubs, parents can connect with the teacher and get answers to questions or share information about their needs, administrators are able to connect to teachers and support students openly, and the public can be an authentic audience to the productivity of the school. The flexibility is there by design, for classrooms to use appropriately. The task for teachers is to be clear about what needs they have to fulfill and to select essential website elements to meet those needs. In fact, the classroom website has the flexibility to meet almost any 21st century learning need. Like any thriving marketplace, it continues to grow, evolve, and reinvent itself to meet the needs and desires of its consumers.

This chapter will address the rationale behind creating a digital marketplace and model specific elements for educators just getting started with classroom websites. These elements include building the website shell; populating the website with information, specifically a calendar and a newsletter; and creating a social networking element for students to work in. For those educators who are already using a classroom website, the chapter also includes a discussion on advanced features like video tutorials, the role of Twitter and smartphones, and ways for parents, administrators, and students to access the greater learning network. The student is the central figure in this chapter, and the information and resources that are presented focus on the engagement, motivation, and success of the student.

We begin by looking at the concept of the digital marketplace. As we work through these concepts, visit **go.solution-tree.com/21stcenturyskills** to view sample teachers' classroom websites.

Understanding the Digital Marketplace

Successful teachers have always searched for ways to make authentic connections with their students in order to engage and motivate them to enjoy learning. Twenty-first-century educators realize that students entering classrooms all around the world are different than all the students that preceded them.

The design of the American public school and public school day that began in the 1800s paralleled the American Industrial Revolution. Classrooms in the 21st century still use these industrialized methods. Curriculum and pedagogy have ebbed and flowed over the 20th century, but we are now in a revolutionary time of change in the classroom. Students sitting in rows with the teacher in the front of the classroom as the pillar of knowledge was the common picture during the industrial era, but as Gerald Gutek (2004) notes, "Postmodernists believe we are now in the postindustrial era, in which the factory-assembly modes of production have been replaced by a new age—the information age of high technology and services for them" (p. 122).

Students' access to information through their devices can be an entry point to the change teachers and school leaders need to make in the design of the school day and physical structure of the school itself.

In the 21st century, a young person can learn anything on his or her own if motivated to do so. A student can go to iTunes U inside of Apple's hugely popular iTunes platform and take classes offered from K–12 school districts and universities all around the world. Sal Khan's Khan Academy has built an extensive library of free web-based learning activities, where students can learn basic concepts in any core subject area. An example of this type of student is a young computer engineer who works at the Khan Academy. Her name is Stephanie, and this is her profile:

> Stephanie loves to learn about all kinds of things. At Khan Academy, she wants to help make learning more fun for millions of people. Stephanie graduated from Duke with a B.S. in Electrical and Computer Engineering, but learned most of what she knows from the Internet. (Khan Academy, 2013)

Veteran educators commonly say that 21st century students just aren't the same as when they were in school. Whether educators say this with a shrug of despair or a sense of wonder, 21st century students truly are different because of the globally connected culture in which they are growing up. This culture has digital literacies layered on the basic literacies of the 19th and 20th centuries. These digital literacies are: (1) information gathering and organization, (2) media, (3) global interconnectivity, (4) networking, and (5) digital citizenship (Tolisano, 2012). Educators look for ways to overtly teach and assess these literacies in the modern classroom. Often, the classroom is a hybrid of traditional literacy forms partnered with these new, technology-based literacies, leading teachers to use classroom websites as entry points for 21st century learning. Table 5.1 describes the elements of the digital marketplace.

Table 5.1: Elements of the Digital Marketplace for Learning

Literacies	Elements
Information gathering and organization	Calendars, newsletters, and blog posts
Media	Movies, pictures (captions), podcasts, webisodes, sound clips, and video games
Global interconnectivity	Links to other classrooms, wikis for collaboration, and challenge activities with global partners
Networking	Social networking elements (message walls, like and unlike features, respond and comment features, and "contact us" options)
Digital citizenship	Participation and maintenance of the website as a portal for learning and identity

The shift in the contemporary learning styles of 21st century students makes it imperative that students have a connection to their school-based learning environments. Such a connection has the following features.

- Students can use classroom websites to gain and organize information efficiently, share their learning collaboratively, connect with their network, and explore resources.

- Parents can use classroom websites to gain information, share their resources, connect with the school community, and participate in their children's school learning experiences.

- Teachers can build online meeting places that connect parents to the classroom and provide access to schedules and resources to enable parental support of their students during the learning process.

- Administrators and instructional coaches can collaborate with teachers in the construction of quality webpages to provide students with the most up-to-date and rigorous content that aligns with state and national standards.

- Teachers can design and construct classroom management platforms using free and easy social media–style applications.

Why Teachers Need a Website

"When is that due? Do you know when the next test is?" These are basic questions that teachers hear from students every day. Why not have all the answers to these questions in one place? A classroom website provides a place for students to access class information from any setting where a student, parent, or teacher can connect to the Internet. The students will quickly get into the habit of checking their classroom website if the teacher regularly prompts them to go there to obtain information that has been previously generated in the classroom. These simple prompts gently put responsibility back on the student for accessing information needed to be successful in the classroom.

Philip Vinogradov, a science teacher in suburban Philadelphia, uses Wikispaces (http://wikispaces.com) as the platform for his classroom website. He reinforces the skills of the classroom marketplace by including: (1) individual class portals, (2) online classroom assignments, and (3) video tutorials. Many teachers find that when they construct the framework of their websites and add the initial content for students, the students then have the opportunity to participate in the growth of the website itself. By adding a blog or a message board, the teacher is able to add interactivity to the site. In the Wikispaces platform, the teacher can set up password-protected student pages to allow students to upload content and work collaboratively on projects. In situations where students have limited access to computers, students can still publish their work through the classroom website using school computer labs or public library computers.

Why Parents and Students Need a Website

"Where is that classroom newsletter that Olivia brought home?" Teachers have often distributed classroom newsletters. They have been mailed home at the cost of postage and handling, distributed via the students, or placed in the abyss of the backpack. An electronic newsletter saves the cost of postage, paper, and handling and is a platform where parents can find the same information their children have access to in the classroom. Up-to-date and relevant information posted on the website allows for greater communication between the student and his or her parents about what is happening in school. Teachers can receive and respond to questions from parents about homework assignments, tests, and projects. Using a web-based calendar that is linked to the website, parents can access the schedule of future tests and project due dates. The calendar also links parents to the learning resources the teacher posts for students. Parents who are concerned about the success of their children in school will access a website on a regular basis, providing it has up-to-date schedules and information that helps them support their children's efforts to be successful in school.

Ashley Perry, a science teacher in South Carolina, uses Google Calendar to list her science classroom assignments and test dates. Parents are able to access this information from their phones or any mobile device.

Chris White, a physics teacher in South Carolina, set up his classroom website (www.oconee.k12.sc.us.webpages/cwhite) with a "Miss Class Today?" section with notes for students who are absent or parents who want to review material from the class to support their children's learning. The student is the central focus of the classroom website. In addition, all students' parents, guardians, or mentors can be key stakeholders in the academic success of the children.

Why Administrators Need a Website

"So, how do you get a view into every classroom?" The teacher's classroom website is a portal into the learning environment for administrators who are looking for ways to be active role models. If the principal is the instructional leader of the school, one of his or her 21st century roles is to encourage, guide, and provide a platform for teachers to build a quality website as an instructional tool. The principal can provide regular feedback to teachers in order to keep their websites up to date and relevant to the operational curriculum being delivered. When there is an open line of communication with the principal about policies and new online opportunities that are married to evaluation and performance goals, the teacher's motivation to maintain the website is greater.

District-level instructional leaders, principals, and assistant principals also have the opportunity to model the construction of websites for their teachers by first building their own. Connecting with the school community through a blog or posting news about the success that is taking place in the district's schools allows administrators to model expectations for teachers. For example, the Connected Principals network (http://connectedprincipals.com) is a resource for K–12 principals and instructional leaders, who use it to share information via blogs or school websites. As a result, parents use digital newsletters and calendars to keep apprised of school events, school schedules, and student news.

Building Your Website

Teachers can start the process by reviewing examples of exemplary classroom websites, which they can find using resources like the eduScapes index (http://eduscapes.com). If a school district does not have the funding to provide a website-hosting service for teachers or schools, the teachers and administrators can still construct one using myriad free website-hosting services (see table 5.2). An example of an easy-to-use application for building a website is Yola, which uses a drag-and-drop system to build text and image areas. Google sites like Google Drive and Google Calendar are also popular. Teachers should experiment with sites to find the one that works best.

Table 5.2: Resources to Start a Classroom Website

Resource	Description
Cool Classroom and Educator Pages (http://eduscapes.com/tap/topic60.htm)	Examples for every content area
School District of Oconee County (www.oconee.k12.sc.us)	Specific district sample to model how it can all come together
Yola (http://yola.com)	Free classroom website builder with drag-and-drop process
WordPress (http://wordpress.com)	Free classroom website builder with options to see work in HTML or document-like screen
Google Sites (http://sites.google.com)	Free classroom website builder with user-friendly supports
Weebly for Education (http://education.weebly.com)	Free classroom website builder with education network options

Building an Electronic Calendar

"When is it due?" "I lost my rubric." "What is our homework for tonight?" "When is our next test?" Teachers hear questions like these every day. How often does the teacher hear, "That was due *today*?" or "I didn't know we had a test today." Parents hear similar statements on a regular basis: "I don't have any homework" or "It is not due until next week" or "I forgot to write my homework in my classroom assignments agenda." Maintaining an online classroom calendar can eliminate many of these questions and complaints. No longer can students or parents complain about being misinformed about assignments and due dates. If a teacher establishes an online calendar at the beginning of the school year and updates it regularly, students and parents will become accustomed to finding homework and assignment information online.

What about students who miss class? How can they access the class notes that they missed when they were absent and see when their next assignment is due? A classroom calendar is a great way for students and parents to stay informed of homework, reading assignments, tests and quizzes, due dates, and special events. A calendar that is linked to a teacher website provides the answers to myriad questions in one place. Maintaining a classroom calendar is thus a major component of the classroom website and is the most efficient way to keep the entire learning community informed. An excellent, user-friendly application for teachers who want to build a classroom calendar that can be hyperlinked to their classroom website is Assign-A-Day (http://assignaday.4teachers.org).

Many teachers argue that there is not enough time to maintain a classroom calendar in addition to their other teaching duties. Teachers are under tremendous pressure to meet academic standards, communicate with parents, collaborate with colleagues, grade and return assignments quickly, take classes, and participate in morning, lunch, and afternoon duty—the list goes on and on. A classroom calendar, if done efficiently, should *not* add more time or stress to a teacher's workday. How much time do teachers spend repeating themselves, sending assignments to students who miss class, or answering phone calls from parents about assignments? Having a classroom calendar online and directing students and parents there to obtain information will reduce the amount of time spent doing each of these tasks.

There are many tools available for teachers to create a classroom calendar that can be linked to or embedded in any web-based platform. Most school web-hosting services offer an online calendar, but there are also numerous free online calendars. The electronic calendars listed in table 5.3 can be linked to classroom websites. Teachers can revise them without logging in to the website editing area. Calendars are accessed remotely, and the calendar is automatically updated when the website is refreshed. Resources and web-based materials related to the events posted on these calendars can be hyperlinked directly into the date box on the calendar.

Table 5.3: Examples of Calendars

Resource	Description
Google Calendar (http://calendar.google.com)	Teachers need a Gmail (http://mail.google.com) account, and then they can hyperlink or embed the calendar on their classroom website.
Assign-A-Day (http://assignaday.4teachers.org)	Teachers need a 4Teachers (http://4teachers .org) account, and then they can hyperlink or embed the calendar on their classroom website.

Producing a Paperless Newsletter

At Wendy Groomes's kindergarten classroom website area, the newsletters are hyperlinked for student and parent access. An advantage to the paperless newsletter is the ability to edit, revise, and adjust the information. When dates for assignments, events, or performances change, teachers can update them immediately, rather than having incorrect information on family bulletin boards and refrigerators. Teachers can guide parents in converting from a paper to an electronic newsletter on parent nights and in their regularly scheduled parent conferences, through email, or through notes on the classroom webpage. To support these efforts, teachers can place responsibility in the hands of the students by creating a lesson that will require them to teach their parents to use the classroom website as an information source.

Updating the Classroom Website

How often a teacher updates an online calendar depends on the needs of the teacher and what his or her schedule requires. Some prefer to plan day to day, and some have assignments and due dates planned for an entire school year by August. Most teachers fall somewhere in the middle. It is recommended that teachers post assignments weekly, but some may want to update the calendar once a month. The bottom line is that as long as they post assignments and due dates in a timely manner, teachers can do whatever they prefer.

Building a Social Learning Network

How does the global revolution of the online social network affect American and Canadian teenagers' communication and learning skills? How can educators leverage the power of this 21st century cultural phenomenon to increase student achievement?

The Pew Research Center's Internet & American Life Project reports that teens continue to be avid users of social networking websites. In September 2009, 73 percent of online American teens ages twelve to seventeen used an online social network website—a statistic that has continued to climb upward from 55 percent in November of 2006, and 65 percent in February of 2008 (Lenhart, Purcell, Smith, & Zickuhr, 2010). The most recent results in July of 2011 from the Pew Internet & American Life Project report that 75 percent of children ages twelve to seventeen access a social network website (Lenhart, Purcell, Smith, & Zickuhr, 2012).

All young people have natural instincts to want to fit in and socially connect with their peers. Do you remember passing notes to classmates in school? Did you negotiate with your parents on the use of the home telephone when you were a teenager? The online social network is the 21st century equivalent of passing notes, and mobile communication devices have replaced the landline telephone. The attraction to an online social network for a young person is the readily available connection to peers coupled with the ability to communicate with them instantly.

Marc Prensky (2001) describes the difference between a *digital native* and a *digital immigrant*. The term *digital native* refers to 21st century students who are native speakers of technology, fluent in the digital language of computers, video games, and the Internet. Prensky refers to those of us who were not born into the digital world as *digital immigrants*. We have adopted many aspects of the technology, but just like those who learn another language later in life, we retain an accent, because we still have one foot in the past. The teacher who is a digital immigrant may tend to view students' online social networking as a distraction, while the digital native views it as a way for students to learn about the world and each other (Prensky, 2001).

The fact is that teachers and school leaders have a tremendous opportunity to harness the power of the social learning community to connect learning activities together outside of the classroom. A variety of social network types of platforms is available. There are public options such as Facebook and Twitter, just to name two. There are also non-public options that are available to teachers. These can be built into or connected with the classroom websites and used as class discussion areas and for document sharing. The digital natives will connect seamlessly into social networks for learning because they are natural forms of communication for them.

The Power of Connectivism

Maria Pettenati and Maria Cigognini (2007) describe the emerging learning theory *connectivism*. Through connectivism, knowledge is created through the connections people make with each other using online networking technology (Pettenati & Cigognini, 2007). According to this theory, being a knowledgeable person requires the ability to know how to connect with other people and how to find information. One of the essentials of a successful connectivist learning environment is that learning activities must remain current and accurate or the participants lose interest in being connected.

In the fall of 2012, Facebook reached over one billion members, the equivalent to the population of a very large country. In all probability, the site has grown and prospered because its users keep their information current. Facebook (2012) reports that up to 50 percent of its hundreds of millions of active members log in every day. The idea of staying up to date on current knowledge is also a key attribute in the lifelong learning process. It is not hard to tell if someone's Facebook profile is not up to date; it is even more apparent if a teacher's classroom website is not up to date.

Facebook and Myspace are blocked in the majority of public school districts because of the required compliance with the Children's Internet Protection Act (Federal Communications Commission, 2011). E-rate (www.fcc.gov/learnnet) is a government-funded program that discounts certain communications technologies to make them more affordable for eligible schools and libraries (Federal Communications Commission, 2004). In order to receive E-rate discounts on Internet service, public schools and public libraries must comply with CIPA and implement filtering systems to protect students from offensive content. This is the key CIPA statement that affects the use of social networks in schools.

> Schools and libraries subject to CIPA are required to adopt and implement an Internet safety policy addressing: (a) access by minors to inappropriate matter on the Internet; (b) the safety and security of minors when using electronic mail, chat rooms, and other forms of direct electronic communications; (c) unauthorized access, including so-called "hacking," and other unlawful activities by minors online; (d) unauthorized disclosure, use, and dissemination of personal information regarding minors; and (e) measures restricting minors' access to materials harmful to them. (FCC, 2012)

The safety of students is the number-one priority of all teachers and administrators. School leaders face the challenge of balancing student Internet safety with being progressive in providing students with the opportunity to develop their communication and collaboration skills using connectivist learning environments.

Teachers have the option of substituting the traditional classroom website with a portal to their classroom that models a safe and secure social learning network. As of September 2012, the powerful, user-friendly, and free classroom social networking platform Edmodo (www.edmodo.com) had over seven million users, and according to their "about" page, they were connecting over 27 million learners (Edmodo, 2014). Edmodo's security features, which the teacher completely controls, are another reason for its popularity with parents and administrators. In thirty minutes, teachers can have their classes set up in Edmodo and begin the process of allowing their students to join. Students do not need an email address to join, because Edmodo works on a class-code system that the teacher can easily manage.

Edmodo has a Facebook look and feel that is attractive to students. Teachers can guide students as they construct a professional image and biography in the site's robust student profile area. This is an excellent opening activity when students first join. It is also the identification (ID) card for being a good digital citizen in a social network; for young people, a digital identity is an essential part of one's social identity. The use of a classroom website in the form of a social network therefore presents teachers with the opportunity to guide students in building their digital identities as citizens who are going to make a positive contribution to society. Edmodo's parent portal, accessed with a unique parent ID linked to the student's identity, allows parents to access their children's assignments, calendar, and grades.

Free, Secure Text Messaging

Twenty-first-century students use text messaging to communicate, not email (Lenhart, Purcell, Smith, & Zickuhr, 2012). One of the powerful aspects of Edmodo is that it has free, secure text-messaging notifications. Teachers can post an assignment on a Monday, and that assignment is automatically populated on the class's main news page, calendar, and app, available free for students and teachers in the Apple and Android marketplaces.

An alternative with similar features to Edmodo is Schoology (www.schoology .com).

Marketing the Classroom and Using Social Media

Among the most powerful elements of the classroom website are the simple tools that empower teachers to connect with students when they are outside class. The concept of the *flipped classroom*, according to which students are prompted to study and learn content outside of the classroom (Bergmann & Sams, 2012), is easily accomplished with the classroom website. Teachers with quality classroom websites can easily "flip" their classrooms and provide the opportunity for learning outside of school.

The growth of Facebook, Twitter, and texting and the increased capability of cell phones have had a revolutionary impact on the way young people communicate since 2006. In December 2010, Lee Rainie, the director of the Pew Research Center's Internet & American Life Project, reported that Facebook passed Google as the most popular site on the Internet. Two-thirds of online adults are now creating their own content. The ascendance of Facebook highlights the degree to which the online environment has become participatory and social (Mui & Whoriskey, 2010). Teachers are also able to use their classroom websites to prompt their students to write and communicate using the globally popular Twitter microblogging format. For more information, visit teacher networks such as TeachHUB (www.teachhub.com) and explore their articles (for example, "50 Ways to Use Twitter in the Classroom" [Miller, 2012], or visit **go.solution-tree .com/21stcenturyskills** to access the resources mentioned in text).

One classroom website in New York included a challenge: translate scenes from Shakespeare's *Romeo and Juliet* into tweets and the dialogue into texts. Once students posted responses and the teacher approved them, the students were able to rate the postings for clarity. Students began to note where comprehension was lost or compromised when student authors tried to be concise. Students were tweeting their entries and pushing one another to improve. Parents even got involved and wanted the school to produce a modern version of *Romeo and Juliet* with the new dialogue from the tweets and texts. All this learning was created as a byproduct from this challenge activity on the classroom website.

This assignment was outside the classroom; it was not graded or a part of the seat time in school. Yet, it had a huge impact on student engagement, networking, and revision practices. The students asked if they could translate essays from different assignments into tweets and evaluate comprehension lost the same way they did for the *Romeo and Juliet* assignment. This activity is a perfect example of the power of the marketplace for learning.

Because schools block many of the social media platforms, teachers must be creative in implementing social media–style communication. For example, a teacher can set up his or her own Twitter-style message board using TodaysMeet (http:// todaysmeet.com) and use the examples shared on the "50 Ways to Use Twitter in the Classroom" (Miller, 2012) to prompt the students to communicate Twitter style. This resource has numerous activities to stimulate students to tell stories, share opinions, and even write poetry using Twitter's 140-character microblogging format.

Conclusion

A portal into the classroom is essential for learning. Now is the time for K–12 teachers and administrators to design a virtual meeting place for all who are involved in the success of each student. This chapter shared a variety of methods and resources for teachers to do so, but the tools and applications available to teachers increase every day.

According to the marketplace concept, the classroom website can be used in a multitude of flexible and purposeful ways. The ability to share, connect, reflect, and create together in this way is leading all of us to new forms of learning in this place called school. This is your invitation to build your own website designed to support the learning you are leading.

You are challenged to model the learning that you are doing.

References and Resources

Bergmann, J., & Sams, A. (2012). *Flip your classroom: Reach every student in every class every day.* Eugene, OR: International Society for Technology in Education.

Facebook. (2012). *Facebook statistics.* Accessed at http://investor.fb.com/releasedetail .cfm?ReleaseID=802760 on November 1, 2013.

Federal Communications Commission. (2011). *Children's Internet Protection Act (CIPA) (2011).* Accessed at www.fcc.gov/guides/childrens-internet-protection-act on November 1, 2013.

Federal Communications Commission. (2004). *E-rate.* Accessed at http://transition .fcc.gov/learnnet on November 1, 2012.

Federal Communications Commission. (2012). *Guide: Children's Internet Protection Act.* Accessed at www.fcc.gov/cgb/consumerfacts/cipa.html on November 1, 2012.

Groomes, W. (2012). *Northside Elementary School, Seneca, South Carolina: School District of Oconee County.* Accessed at www.oconee.k12.sc.us/webpages /WGroomes on November 1, 2012.

Gutek, G. L. (2004). *Philosophical and ideological voices in education.* Boston: Allyn & Bacon.

Khan Academy. (2013). *About: Our team.* Accessed at www.khanacademy.org/about /the-team on June 5, 2013.

Lenhart, A., Purcell, K., Smith, A., & Zickuhr, K. (2010). *Social media and young adults: Part 3: Social media—Teens and online social networks.* Washington, DC: Pew Internet & American Life Project. Accessed at www.pewinternet.org /Reports/2010/Social-Media-and-Young-Adults/Part-3/1-Teens-and-online-social -networks.aspx?r=1 on November 1, 2012.

Lenhart, A., Purcell, K., Smith, A., & Zickuhr, K. (2012). *Social media and young adults: Teens and Privacy Management Survey 2012.* Washington, DC: Pew Internet & American Life Project. Accessed at www.pewinternet.org/~/media /Files/Questionnaire/2012/SurveyQuestions_ParentsTeensAndOnlinePrivacy.pdf on November 1, 2013.

Miller, S. (2012). *50 ways to use Twitter in the classroom.* Accessed at www.teachhub .com/50-ways-use-twitter-classroom on November 1, 2012.

Mui, Y. Q., & Whoriskey, P. (2010, December 31). Facebook passes Google as most popular site on the Internet, two measures show. *The Washington Post*. Accessed at www.pewinternet.org/Media-Mentions/2010/Facebook-passes-Google-as-most -popular-site-on-the-Internet.aspx on December 31, 2010.

Pettenati, M. C., & Cigognini, M. E. (2007). Social networking theories and tools to support connectivist learning activities. *International Journal of Web-Based Learning and Teaching Technologies, 2*(3), 42–60.

Prensky, M. (2001). Digital natives, digital immigrants. *On the Horizon, 9*(5). Accessed at www.marcprensky.com/writing/Prensky%20-%20Digital%20 Natives,%20Digital%20Immigrants%20-%20Part1.pdf on August 8, 2013.

Seneca High School. (n.d.). *Teacher websites*. Accessed at www.oconee.k12.sc.us /classroompages.cfm?location=12 on November 1, 2012.

Teacher Tap. (2012). *Cool classroom & educator pages*. Accessed at http://eduscapes .com/tap/topic60.htm on November 1, 2012.

Tolisano, S. R. (2012). *Upgrade your lesson—21st century literacies*. Accessed at http:// langwitches.org/blog/wp-content/uploads/2012/02/Upgrade-21st-century-skills -literacies-KWHALQ-TEMPLATE.pdf on November 1, 2013.

Index